Praise for Sherri Brooks Vinton

"*Eat It Up!* assembles America's long-lost kitchen resourcefulness into a practical, punchy package. Sherri's recipes and worldview—not to mention her fridgeview—will have you converting would-be wasted food into new dishes in no time. And through that thrifty shift, *Eat It Up!* will pay for itself in mere weeks!"

—Jonathan Bloom, author of *American Wasteland*

"Amidst increasing recognition of the dramatic scope and adverse impacts of food waste, *Eat It Up!* offers readers some of the most effective—and delicious—ways to effect change. By providing tips and techniques for buying, storing, and preparing foods, along with a plethora of root-to-frond, nose-to-tail, and leftover-to-delicacy recipes, the book empowers home cooks to prepare tasty meals while protecting the environment, saving money, and conserving the invaluable resource of food."

—Chris Hunt, Special Advisor on Food and Agriculture,
GRACE Communications Foundation

"*The Real Food Revival* is a compelling, comprehensive, and cannily written A-to-Z guide for interacting with the multifaceted, often convoluted business of food. A much needed work of integrity and hope."

—Dan Barber, chef/owner of Blue Hill and Blue Hill at Stone Barns

"*Put 'em Up!* is exactly what a lot of us need right now: some good guidance on how to preserve that summer harvest we've grown to love and want to experience throughout the year. What a delicious way to eat locally even when the snow is falling."

—Deborah Madison, author of *The New Vegetarian Cooking for Everyone* and
Local Flavors: Cooking and Eating from America's Farmers' Markets

"The Local Food movement has created a whole community of food and farm enthusiasts, shopping locally, even growing their own. With *Put 'em Up!*, Sherri takes it one step further and teaches us how to extend the harvest and have local, delicious treats all year long!"

—Nena Johnson, former director of Public Programs,
Stone Barns Center for Food and Agriculture

"Compelling ideas on taking your homemade goods from the jar to the plate."

—Sean Timberlake, Founder, Punk Domestics

"Sherri's books are the finest, most aptly detailed guides to food preservation that I know and use."

—Gary Nabhan, author of *Coming Home to Eat*

"Buying an apple can be a revolutionary act. Don't believe it? Read *The Real Food Revival*."

—Andrea Sachs, *Time*

"At once evocative and utilitarian, the book is destined to become a must-have resource for the real food movement as it shows how simple and delicious these safe, proven methods of food preservation really are. Whether you love to cook or are afraid to cook, buy this book!"

—Kurt Michael Friese, chef and author of
A Cook's Journey: Slow Food in the Heartland

"*The Real Food Revival* tells you what is wrong with our food—why it is less delightful than it should be. It also tells you what you can about it—and supplies the two essential, all-too-rare ingredients: truth and hope."

—Margaret Visser, author of *Much Depends on Dinner*

"*Put 'em Up!* demystifies something our grandmothers used to do and offers a straight-forward way to doing something that can add real richness to our lives."

—Josh Viertel, former president, Slow Food USA

"Preserving food is the epitome of truly understanding the whole picture of fresh, local, and support of seasonal farming and cooking. Sherri's book, *Put 'em Up*! may just have a permanent place on my home and restaurant counters. . . . This book is full of practical and delicious ideas. . . ."

—Chef and author Jesse Ziff-Cool

"A blissful combination of old-fashioned preserving know-how and contemporary taste. Easy, detailed instructions . . . ideas organized by each fruit or vegetable you find at the farmer's market; and inspired recipes. . . . *Put 'em Up!* is the perfect way to save and savor the best of the season year round."

—Anne Bramley, host of the Eat Feed podcast
and author of *Eat Feed Autumn Winter*

EAT IT UP!

Also by Sherri Brooks Vinton

Put 'em Up!
Put 'em Up! Fruit
The Put 'em Up! Preserving Answer Book
The Real Food Revival (with Ann Clark Espuelas)

EAT IT UP!

150 Recipes to Use Every Bit and Enjoy
Every Bite of the Food You Buy

SHERRI BROOKS VINTON

Da Capo
LIFE
LONG

A Member of the Perseus Books Group

Designed by Jack Lenzo
Set in Eames Century Modern by the Perseus Books Group

Library of Congress Cataloging-in-Publication Data
Names: Vinton, Sherri Brooks, 1968- author.
Title: Eat it up! : how to save time, money, and the planet by enjoying every
  last bite of the food you buy / Sherri Brooks Vinton.
Description: Boston, MA : Da Capo Lifelong Books, a member of the Perseus
  Books Group, [2016] | Includes bibliographical references and index.
Identifiers: LCCN 2015045183| ISBN 9780738218182 (pbk.) | ISBN 9780738218199
  (e-book)
Subjects: LCSH: Food conservation. | Food waste—Prevention. | Cooking. |
  LCGFT: Cookbooks.
Classification: LCC TX357 .V55 2016 | DDC 641.5—dc23 LC record available at http://lccn.loc
.gov/2015045183

First Da Capo Press edition 2016

Published by Da Capo Press
A Member of the Perseus Books Group
www.dacapopress.com

Da Capo Press books are available at special discounts for bulk purchases in the U.S. by corporations, institutions, and other organizations. For more information, please contact the Special Markets Department at the Perseus Books Group, 2300 Chestnut Street, Suite 200, Philadelphia, PA, 19103, or call (800) 810-4145, ext. 5000, or e-mail special.markets@perseusbooks.com.

10 9 8 7 6 5 4 3 2 1

For every meal, every sip, every bite, I am grateful.

CONTENTS

3: The Whole Beast

111

4: Pantry

5: A Little Extra—Upcycling

INTRODUCTION

As I write, I am living in my new home state, California, where we are going through an extended drought. Water is becoming an increasingly precious commodity. The majority of water used in the state—80 percent of it—goes to the field, and the drought is putting extreme pressure on farmers here who need to irrigate their crops. This is not just a California problem. An estimated 50 percent of the fruit and vegetables and much of the milk and meat consumed in the United States is produced in California and shipped across the country. If California fields remain dry, our national food supply will be affected.

This very real and pressing issue brings into high relief the connection between our natural resources and a stable food supply. You need good, clean land, air, and water to have good, clean food. The reverse is true as well. Squandering our supply of good, clean food wastes our precious natural resources.

Drive by the expansive fields of many of California's biggest growers and the waste is apparent. I came face to face with a prime example this spring as we drove through cauliflower fields where the plants were being harvested. Cauliflower heads are plucked from the center of the plant, the abundant wreath of nutritious leaves that surround it—pounds of fresh, nutritious food—are left to rot on the ground. They're readily available and taste great, but there's no market for them, so they go uneaten. As do many of the by-products of our modern food chain that favors easy to transport, long lasting, perfect-looking produce and the filet, the pretty center, the unchallenging cut of meat.

We eaters can change this trend of frivolous waste and preserve our natural resources. And we don't need to lobby Congress, picket wasteful growers, or stand up to industrial agriculture to do it. We can change the world by simply changing what we have for dinner. By eating the normally cast-off foods—the cauliflower leaves you might get from your grower at the farmers' market, the greens from your beets, the stems from your broccoli, and more—you play an instrumental role in creating a more efficient, more abundant food supply.

Kitchen efficiency is not a trend. It is one of the basic principles of home economy, allowing home cooks to turn out great-tasting meals without breaking the family bank. Step back in time to any grandmother's kitchen and you would see many of the ideas in this book in action. Stale bread isn't discarded—it's drenched in egg custard and sizzled in butter for a luxurious tasting breakfast of Pain Perdu. Bones from Sunday's roast don't hit the waste bin until every last bit of their flavor is simmered into a big pot of broth.

Step into any professional kitchen that's manned by chefs who are worth their salt and you will see food utility not only in action but raised to an art form. Chef Dan Barber drew attention to the delicious potential of many of the unused and "ignored and uncoveted" foods, as he describes them, in his temporary pop-up restaurant, wastED, in New York City. Dan and an array of top chefs from around the world put together menus that turned everything from the peels and pulp from fruits and vegetables to used coffee grounds and odd cuts of fish and meat into meals that had diners swooning over dishes that illustrated "how we can change our ways of cooking and eating to feed a growing population."

You don't need to be a granny or a chef. You don't need to go Dumpster diving or field gleaning to be a part of a better, more delicious food future. You just need to enjoy your food. Right down to the last crunchy crust, the last berry on the bush, the last lick of the pot—every last bite of it.

Sound daunting? It doesn't have to be. You don't need to do everything listed in this book all the time. Start small. Pick one tip or recipe and give it a try. You don't need to run a zero-waste kitchen to make a huge difference. Every bit you save takes a bite out of food waste.

WHAT'S UP WITH EATING IT UP?

THE WHY AND HOW OF REDUCING FOOD WASTE IN YOUR HOME KITCHEN

I love good food. Well-raised food. Local, seasonal food that reflects environment and culture and tradition. And I will go to great lengths to get my hands on it. CSA memberships, farm stands, farmers' markets, and trusted third-party vendors—I always find a way to track delicious eats. Good food means something to me. That rustic, slightly gnarled bunch of carrots isn't just rabbit food—it's a farmer's hard work, well-tended soil, good clean water, and days of warm sun that I hold in my hand. And now that I have it home, it's lunch.

Having been a farm groupie for some time now, perhaps my feelings about well-raised food run a little more deeply than they do for most. And that's okay. You don't have to wax poetic about your groceries to want to get the most out of the food you bring home. Enjoying every last bite of the food you buy makes sense for a lot of different reasons. Here are just a few:

REASONS TO EAT IT UP!

Saves Money

Food costs. Throw out your food and you're throwing out your money. It's hard to imagine buying new clothes, coming home, and throwing half of them away, yet that's what many of us do with our food. Maybe not all at once, but a little bit at a time. And it adds up. I sometimes catch myself as I'm about to toss out something that represents a relatively small percentage of my total grocery bill, such as leftover rice. It's easy to just pitch it, but by doing so I'm getting less for the money.

Half of last night's rice, a few bites of chicken, a handful of broccoli florets. That amount of food is often discarded without a second thought. But when you stop to look at it, you haven't just thrown out a bite of this and that. Sauté it up with an onion and maybe some sesame oil and you've got dinner. Save those bits and bobs and you haven't just saved the cost of the leftovers, but the cost of the new meal you didn't have to make. Eating it up, saves it up. After all, no one ever got rich by wasting money . . . or food.

Saves Time

We're busy people with busy lives. Who wouldn't want an extra slice of time in their week? Using up what you have on hand can mean more efficient trips to the market. Utilizing leftovers from last night's dinner gives you a running start on tonight's meal prep. Eat it up and you'll spend less time buying and cooking it up.

Tastes Great

There's no sustainable kitchen practice that's worth a fig if it doesn't lead to a tasty meal. Food is about pleasure, first and foremost. Although there are a lot of reasons to support local agriculture—from environmental to social to economic—I was lured into the Real Food movement by my taste buds. Locally raised, in-season, fresh-from-the-field grub is the tastiest you will find. When I'm eating up every last bite of the food I have in my kitchen, I'm not thinking, *Oh, clever frugal me*; I'm thinking, *Dang, that looks tasty.*

I can remember my Granny Toni giving the jar of her home-canned tomatoes a swish with a little water and pouring it into whatever sauce she was making. I made some wisecrack about her being such a penny-pincher and she said to me, "It's not just the money, it's the flavor. You've got to get all the flavor into the pot." I think of that every time I take the extra effort to get to the dregs of the jam jar, the last bit of pickle juice in the crock. Don't waste it, taste it!

Preserves Natural Resources

It takes a lot to grow food. A lot of water, a lot of energy, a lot of fresh air and sunshine. Every step in the process—from planting the seeds to weeding to harvesting and shipping—is quite resource intensive. Machinery needs to be powered. Fields are irrigated. Crops are transported. Even the most sustainably run farm uses natural resources to produce the good food that fills our plates. By enjoying every last bite of the food that comes out of this process, we lower the resource-to-calorie quotient. Eat it up and you'll be doing your part to use but not waste the air, water, soil, and energy it takes to grow our crops.

Honors the Farmers' Hard Work

Accountant, marketer, customer service representative, advertising exec, machinist, weather forecaster, ecologist, community organizer—these are just some of the jobs that a modern farmer needs to be expert at these days.

Oh, and having the ability to actually grow food. And not just make it come out of the ground but do it well. That means properly prepping the soil so the carrots grow straight, knowing the exact moment to harvest broccoli before it bolts, curing the sweet potatoes so they don't rot, understanding the positive effects of frost on parsnips, puzzling out your fields with underplantings and crop rotations that not only maximize the space, but encourage fertility and more. And doing all those things before many of us have even had our first cup of coffee. It's not just hard work, it's incredible shape-shifting, mystical, miracle-making stuff. The best way to honor the blood, sweat, and tears it takes to fill your market basket? Eat it. Every bite of it.

Maximizes Farmland Productivity

More people means we need to grow more food, right? Well, how about instead of growing more, we just eat what's already there. Americans only consume about half of the food that comes off our fields. Simple math, we can have about twice as much food without planting a single acre more, if we just eat what we grow.

WHERE DOES IT ALL GO?

With so many great reasons to enjoy every last bite, it's hard to believe that, according to the National Resources Defense Council (NRDC), 40 percent of all food produced in the United States is discarded. Through our production and distribution methods to our commercial and home practices, we waste twice as much food as we did in the 1970s. As the world's population expands, the knee-jerk reaction is to grow more. But I say: before we plant more crops, let's eat what we've already sown. If we reduced our food waste by only 15 percent, we could feed 25 million Americans. Reduce it by 30 percent and we would have enough food to nourish the 50 million Americans that identify as food-insecure. Is food waste an easy problem to solve? Not entirely. But there are some simple steps we all can take to utilize more of the harvest.

It's important to keep in mind that food waste isn't just scraps. Reducing it doesn't mean that you'll be eating anything that isn't perfectly wholesome and delicious. The fact is that the majority of the food we waste isn't spoiled or inferior, it's perfectly good food that is simply discarded along the food chain. Here are some of the ways that we lose what we grow:

In the Field

A lot of our food never makes it off the farm. It's the misshapen tomato in the field that the packer won't accept because it's not picture-perfect. The crop that's left in the ground because a glut in the market has dropped the price of the food so low that it is no longer profitable to harvest it. It's the secondary crop, such as broccoli and cauliflower leaves that haven't found a market. It's the orchard of apples left unpicked because the farmer could not find the labor to pick it. In these ways and more valuable food is wasted right where it is grown.

In Processing and Packing

Produce again enters into a beauty contest in the processing and packing phase of distribution. Packers adhere to strict appearance standards when grading produce for distribution. Food that doesn't look pretty is downgraded or discarded. Edible carrots that aren't perfectly straight, for example, are often kept out of the marketplace because they don't meet industry standards for appearance. Perfectly delicious food that can't find a buyer at the retail level or that won't bring enough profit to the packer, perhaps because there is a glut of supply, can be discarded as well.

In the Store

Retail shelves are kept fully stocked—above the amount that is expected to be sold—to present a picture of abundance that is attractive to the shopper. The overstocking practice causes food to bruise from the weight of the display and overhandling as shoppers repeatedly pick through the pile, leading to a high percentage of waste.

In the Home

Americans throw out about half of the food that they bring home. Some of it spoils before it is eaten. Some is tossed because it has passed the sell-by date on the carton. A lot of our food hits the bin after it's prepared, either as un-eaten portions on our plate or leftovers that go idle in the fridge.

WHAT CAN YOU DO ABOUT IT?

In this book, we're going to deal with the food waste issue that we, as eaters, have the most control over—in our homes. There are a number of ways to re-duce food waste on the consumer end. Even if you don't do every one of these, all the time, your small changes can make a big difference. Here's a start:

Buy Directly from the Grower

At every point in the food chain, there's another chance for "shrink," or "shrinkage," as the grocery industry calls it—the percentage of food that is spoiled, damaged, or simply discarded along the path from field to point of purchase. Shorten the chain by buying directly from farmers and you mini-mize those opportunities for waste.

Buy Ugly Food

Good, wholesome food is always a beautiful thing to behold, but not always in "straight off the pages of a food mag" kind of way. Some produce may have a shade of uneven coloring or be a tad misshapen. Tastes just as good, but maybe looks a little less than lovely. Such items are often sold by farmers as "seconds" at a discount price and are a great way to get good food for less. And though a harder sell for the farmer, such produce items are a prized treat for the buyer in the know who seeks out substance above style.

Look for Heirloom Produce

Heirloom produce—those varieties that have been passed down through generations of farmers—is grown for its taste, rather than its appearance. The tastiest tomato may very well not be the perfectly shaped, Stop sign red, iconic fruit but, rather, the "cat-faced" sample, as food-lovers call them, with its uneven lumps and bumps and shaded coloring. In fact, many of the heirloom varieties of produce have much more flavor than their commer-cial counterparts but aren't grown industrially because their odd shapes and sizes do not suit the automated equipment used in giant scale operations. You, however, not needing widget-shaped foods suited for standardized machinery, can enjoy all the oddly colored, lopsided but delicious produce that you can get your hands on.

Eat "Trash Fish"

"Trash fish" are not fish from the garbage bin, they are simply fish that rarely make it to the table for any number of reasons. Most often the term is used to describe lesser-known but perfectly tasty fish that haven't gained the popularity of such species as cod, salmon, or tuna, so they don't get ordered by name. Trash fish, such as dogfish, which resembles a meatier version of cod and is just as tasty, has yet to find its audience. So, until it does, it's considered a trash fish—a hard sell. Trash fish is also used to describe "by-catch," the fish that are discarded from the day's take because they weren't the intended catch. Fish that get caught up in shrimp nets or simply weren't the targeted species are examples of by-catch, and although perfectly edible, are most often tossed back into the water dead and dying. According to Oceana, by-catch may represent 40 percent of the global fishing intake—a shocking volume of waste.

Eating trash fish creates a market that is more flexible and less wasteful. So, when your fishmonger offers you something that you've never heard of before, why not give it a go? After all, no one wanted Patagonian toothfish until it was renamed Chilean sea bass. And when your creative chef buys up the random fish hauled back with the day's scallop harvest because he or she would rather see them in a stew than tossed overboard, dig in. Trash fish is good fish.

Organize Your Fridge to Reduce Spoilage

Out of sight, out of mind. I can't tell you how many times I've meant to eat it, I've planned to eat it, I've wanted to eat it, but I just forgot it was there. A tasty bit of cheese in the back of the drawer, three lovely steamed shrimp, half a cup of caramel sauce—how could I forsake you? To avoid losing valuable bites to the chaos of the fridge, it helps to have a system. Try some of these tips:

- **All leftovers live on one shelf.** Visit it first before making your next dinner plan or shopping list, to see what you can eat up.

- **It's a date.** Take a tip from the pros and label all leftovers or opened containers with a "made on" or "opened on" date. Keeping a roll of painter's tape and a marker in a nearby drawer makes it easy.

- **Squirrel it away.** Bought the big size because it was half the price? It's not savings if you throw it out. When possible, section off the portion you can use right away and put the rest in the freezer. Works great for hard cheeses, family packs of meat and fish, cream cheese, butter, pasta sauce, breads, and cakes, and even keeps grains and flours fresher, longer.

- **Delicate on top.** Sturdy produce, such as carrots, celery, apples, and broccoli, can live at the bottom of the crisper very happily. Layer more delicate items, such as peppers, peaches, and summer squashes that might bruise or crush on top of those. Lettuces, herbs, and other leafy items should be on the very top. Eat down through the layers.

- **Don't show your perishables the door.** Sure, it's convenient to have the milk and eggs on the door for easy access, but it doesn't guarantee the longest shelf life. Through the constant opening and closing, the items on the door see the highest temperatures. If you have a high turnover of milk and eggs, you might not notice a difference, but if those items are going off before you can enjoy them, you might relocate them to a cooler compartment. Leave the door for the much less perishable hot sauce.

- **Keep dairy on the low down.** Yogurt, sour cream, and milk do best on the lower shelves of the fridge, where the air is colder.

- **Keep meat on the way low down.** Meat should be stored at the lowest point in the fridge, preferably in a meat drawer if your fridge has one. Not only are the lowest shelves the coldest (cold air sinks), but you don't want the juices from these items to drip on and contaminate any of your other refrigerated foods.

Understand the Shelf Life of Food

Some eaters keep their food until it is much too old. Other eaters throw it out way too soon. The key to reducing food waste in the kitchen is to know the half-life of the food you eat. No one wants to pitch food that's fit to eat, but push that line too much and you could get yourself sick. The dates on the package can be informative, but don't always have the precise info you need (see page 11 for information on package dating).

Good thing your senses give the best clues to rot, particularly when it comes to raw food. Unless it is contaminated from the start by food-borne pathogens picked up in the field or in processing, spoilage makes itself known. If that jar of marmalade is growing a beard, the smell of your milk turns your stomach, that pork chop feels slimy, it's got to go. There is no cooking or preserving process that can redeem it.

Cooked foods have expiration dates, too. A good rule of thumb about cooked food that I learned when getting my food handler's certification was that cooked food is generally safe for up to five days, except for shellfish, which is wholesome for three days after cooking. So, that means that all those "Seven days of post-Thanksgiving leftovers" may be stretching it a bit far. And some dishes may lose flavor or texture even sooner, so always look to your recipe for storage tips.

More detailed information about food spoilage is readily available online. Apps and websites make it easy to look up the life expectancy of any number of foods. You can start here: Still Tasty (http://www.stilltasty.com) is a website and app created by a cooperative effort of the USDA, FDA, and CDC that offers shelf life and storage dates for thousands of food items. You'll also find more information on expiration and sell-by dates (and what they really mean) on page 11.

All food will stay fresher, longer in a fridge that is kept at its chilly best. Food spoils very rapidly at 40°F and above, so you want to stay well below that without getting to a frosty 32°F; 35/36°F is usually a good setting that will compensate for regular opening and closing of the door.

Wrap It Up

Air is a spoiler. It can dry out moist foods, make dry food stale, and carries pathogens. To improve the shelf life of your food, it's best to keep it under wraps.

Cover items that go in the fridge. I am not a big fan of copious amounts of disposable wraps in the kitchen, so I often opt to cover my refrigerated foods in a reusable way. You can use reusable containers. Or you can use the dishes you already have on hand to do the trick. I slide a plate over filled bowls and use bowls as cloches to cover plates of food. An inexpensive set of clear plates and bowls doubles as extra serving and mixing pieces and make it easy to see what's on hand.

Dry goods and snacks, such as cereals, grains, cookies, and crackers, suffer from exposure to air as well. Big rubber bands and clothespins are great for securing original packaging after opening. I store opened bagged items, such as beans and rice, in large canning jars to prevent exposure to air and keep pests away. For cookies and crackers, is there anything cuter than an old-fashioned or even newfangled breadbox, cookie jar, or cracker canister? Keeping one on the counter keeps food fresh and handy.

Label It

It's not just for refrigerated items. Label all cooked and opened food with the date that it was prepared or unpackaged. Keeping a roll of painter's tape and a permanent marker in the kitchen drawer makes it a snap.

CAN I EAT THAT? GOOD VS. BAD MOLD

Mold seems like it would be a pretty clear indicator of spoilage, but the line of good vs. bad mold can be blurry. In some foods, such as cheese, charcuterie, beer, and pickles certain bacteria are introduced or encouraged to colonize to abate other, pathogenic strains and to develop the flavor of the food. For example, the colonies of *Penicillium* that constitute the blue veins of Roquefort are good for the cheese as they keep contamination at bay during the aging process and they taste good, too.

Spontaneous mold development, however, is not always a good thing. I've heard a number of eaters tell stories of their grandmothers simply peeling back the furry mold from a jar of jam and digging in. I don't recommend it. Not all mold is beneficial and the mold you see is not the whole story. Mold isn't just something that lives on the surface; it runs deep with rootlike structures that reach down into soft foods. Moldy yogurt, for example, isn't just spoiled where you see patches of fuzz— the spores extend down into the container. If it's furry, best to pitch it.

One exception to this rule—hard cheeses. Such food products are too dense for surface mold to penetrate. Surface bloom on these items, unless it is black mold, can be safely scraped off and the rest of the cheese can be enjoyed. Spontaneous mold blooms on other fresh or cooked foods are an indication of spoilage.

Know Your Labels

Okay, prepare to have your mind blown. The "expiration" dates on your food are not guarantees that your food is fresh. They are indicators of peak quality and suggested display times for retailers.

"Use by," "Best by," and "Best before," indicate the last date that the manufacturer guarantees quality. Not *safety*, but *quality*. These labels are usually reserved for nonperishables, such as jams, mustards, and sauces that will naturally start to separate or discolor with age. The product may very well be fine to eat (i.e., unnoticeably different) after this date—a long time after this date in fact—but the manufacturer will no longer stand behind it. For example: an unopened bottle of olives past its date may be a little paler in color than you expect when you open it. While they may be fine to eat, you will no longer be able to send them back to the manufacturer, complaining of their mild hue.

Sell-by dates are often used on perishables, such as milk and meat. This is the last date that the product can be displayed for retail, as suggested by the manufacturer. Think of it as a guide, but not a hard-and-fast rule. Grocers may still sell the product after its sell-by date and you may still enjoy it. For example, a carton of milk will be taken off the shelf on its sell-by date, but is still wholesome until sometime after that date—seven to ten days for reduced-fat versions and five to seven days for whole milk.

The exception here is baby food and formula. These items have dates that indicate expiration that one should always heed.

Utilize the Whole Foods You Buy

I am convinced that eaters throw out a good portion of the food they buy because they don't even know it is edible. I was at the farmers' market a while back and handed the farmer several fennel to ring up for me. He proceeded to twist off the stalks and fronds and hand me back just the bulbs. When I questioned him about taking half of my food for himself he laughed and said he just assumed that I wanted them trimmed; everyone did. And miss half the fun? No, thanks. Same with beets and their greens, carrots and their tops, and on and on. That's the fun of good food, eating it up, and you'll find lots of tips for this waste-saving measure in the book.

Eat Up Your Leftovers

And if you overcook? No reason to pitch that little extra this and that. Up-cycle it! As a matter of fact, a handful of cooked veg or protein can make for a whole new meal if you know how to do it. There are a number of recipes at the end of this book to get you started.

Understand Stale vs. Garbage Pail

Age is not necessarily a bad thing (and I don't just mean in women and wine).

Just because a food isn't at its peak of freshness doesn't mean it has to be tossed in the bin. Stale bread makes fantastic Panzanella (page 188). Celery that is beginning to wilt can be refreshed in an ice bath. Old wine? We call that vinegar. Throughout this book, you'll find loads of tips for getting a second life out of good food.

FREEZING

I often use the freezer to buy myself some extra time—it extends shelf life simply and easily. From a crust of bread to a few berries that I know I won't get to in time to some extra soup, duck fat, or half a jar of BBQ sauce that I know I will love to have . . . later. I have some specialized containers for the purpose. You know the ones—inexpensive, washable, reusable, stackable. I use freezer bags, too. Lay them flat when you put them in the freezer, so you can stack them efficiently. I also use a fair amount of glass jars as well. Canning jars are fine in the freezer. They have an extra-thick glass that holds up well under freezing temps. Just be sure not to fill them to the top, to allow for your contents to expand—maybe ½ inch for small jars, and up to an inch for quart-size.

Compost

And when the last little tasty morsels have been gleaned from your groceries and you're left with the truly done and inedible, pile it up, let it rot, and plant it again to grow another great meal. The end of one road can be the beginning of another if you compost your scraps. Sound a bit too *Little House on the Prairie*? You don't need to be a pioneer to do it—you just need the spirit. Compost buckets, bins, and barrels come in a wide range of sizes—from "urban" small (for under the counter or in the corner of the tiniest of studio apartments) to "homesteading" mammoth (to create enough compost for all your garden beds and then some).

Don't want to do it yourself? Many towns and cities are creating municipal composting programs. San Francisco's is mandatory. And if you don't want a DIY solution or your town hasn't gotten on board the compost train just yet, check in with your local farmers' market. Many markets, such as New York City's Greenmarkets, are implementing "back to the farm" programs that will return residential food scraps with the growers to turn into this valuable, nutrient dense fertilizer. See Resources (page 223) for more info on getting the good rot.

2  NOSE-TO-TAIL PRODUCE

"Nose-to-tail" is a concept that's become pretty popular among farm-to-table eaters who are dedicated to enjoying every cut of the animals that are raised for food. But what about produce? Many of the leaves and fronds, stems and skins of our fruits and vegetables are not only edible—they're delicious. Yet many eaters have never learned how to fully utilize the plants that are grown for our plates.

Perhaps it's because many more of us are shopping at local farmers' markets where the whole plant is often sold intact. Or because grocery stores are carrying more of the plant parts, such as broccoli leaves, that were previously discarded. Or we're just getting back to a more practical approach to cooking. But whole plant eating is gaining ground and that's good news all around.

Here's an A–Z (or A–W, apples to watermelon rind!) of terrific ideas for enjoying parts of your produce that you might normally pitch. Don't think of this as Dumpster diving—there's nothing weird or unpalatable here. Think of it more as hidden treasure—previously undiscovered taste that's been at your fingertips all along.

Apple Peels

The iconic apple. Of your eye, as American as, taken once a day, or seductive enough to ruin Eve, apples are a fruit whose mythology looms large. And so does their list of uses—fry them into fritters, bake them into pies and tarts, dip them in caramel, press them into cider, eat them straight out of hand and on and on. As growers plant an increasing number of heirloom varieties— some of which haven't been in production since our grandparents' time—the snacking, baking, and storage options continue to expand. Whether you pick them yourself or just pick them up at your local market, apples are a favorite.

Buying: Wax on, wax off: this is something important to think about when you are enjoying your apples, particularly the peels. Most groceries wax the fruit so that it stays fresh looking on the shelf for a long time. I try to avoid waxed fruits as much as possible by purchasing my apples directly from the farmer or a trusted market that doesn't treat its produce this way. If you find yourself stuck with waxed apples, you'd do best to remove as much of it as possible before diving into any of these recipes. To do this, fill a large bowl with warm water and add a few drops of fragrance-free dish soap or a tablespoon or two each of lemon juice and baking soda. Roll the apples around for a minute or two and then scrub them with a soft-bristled brush. Rinse, dry, and proceed with your recipe.

Storing: Whether you are dealing with waxed or unwaxed fruit, the best way to store your apples is in a cool, dark place. That can be a root cellar, a cool corner of your basement, or your refrigerator's crisper drawer. Wherever you store your apples, keep an eye out for any sign of bruising or rot. It is true that one bad apple will spoil the barrel—the ethylene gas that is produced by ripe and overripe fruits causes the aging process to accelerate in all neighboring produce. So, if you are going to be storing them for the long term, it's best to provide some sort of protective barrier between the apples to help them keep their ethylene to themselves. You can wrap them individually in newspaper or layer them between beds of dried leaves—raked straight from your back-yard—as you load them into your storage container. And be sure to cull any fruit that shows signs of withering—rot travels faster than gossip and will spread from one apple to the next if you let it.

Prepping: There are a lot of ways to skin a lot of things, including apples. You can use a paring knife to slice off the peel—in one long strand if you have that talent. Vegetable peelers are reasonably effective and make safe work for little hands. Or, if you are doing a quantity of fruit, you can invest in a specialized apple peeler or—luxury—a combination apple peeler and corer. These gadgets razor off the peel as the user turns a crank, leaving behind ribbons of spiralized peels—quick, efficient, and kind of fun, too.

Cinnamon Apple Snacks

When I was a kid, I loved to snack on dried apples. These crisps have a lot of great apple flavor, but with the added crunch of the toasted peel. Be sure to cook them thoroughly so they swap their chewy texture for a nice, light snap.

Makes about 1 cup loosely packed dried peels per pound of apples

Peels from 1 to 2 pounds of apples

1 to 2 teaspoons neutral oil, such as organic canola, to coat

1 tablespoon granulated sugar

Pinch or two of ground cinnamon

- Preheat the oven to 250°F.
- Line two baking sheets with parchment paper. In a large bowl, toss the peels with the oil, then the sugar and cinnamon. Arrange in a single layer on the lined baking sheets. Bake for 2½ hours, or until brown and brittle. Let cool completely before serving.
- Can be stored in an airtight container for up to 1 week.

Apple Jelly

This recipe calls for using the whole apple. If you want to use the apple flesh in another recipe and only have the peels and cores, you can substitute a quart of no-sugar-added bottled apple juice or cider plus 1 cup of water for the 4 cups of water called for in the recipe. The pectin, which thickens the jelly, is mostly in the peels and pits of the fruit, so you will still get a good gel.

Makes about 5 cups jelly

4 pounds tart apples (about 12)

3 cups granulated sugar

¼ cup bottled lemon juice

- Wash and stem the apples but leave the peel and core. Roughly chop the apples and put them in a large stockpot. Add enough water to cover the apples, about 4 cups. Bring to a boil over high heat. Lower the heat to medium-low and simmer until tender, about 30 minutes, adding a bit more water, as necessary, to prevent scorching.
- Pour the mixture into a dampened jelly bag, available wherever canning supplies are sold, or a colander lined with dampened cheesecloth set over a 2-quart bowl, and let drain in the refrigerator overnight. Do not press or squeeze the jelly bag or cheesecloth.
- Measure 1 quart of the resulting apple juice and place it in a large saucepan set over high heat. Stir in the sugar and lemon juice. Bring to a full boil that you cannot stir down. Continue to boil until the jelly reaches 220°F on a candy thermometer. Remove from the heat.
- You can cool, refrigerate, and cover the jelly and enjoy it within 3 weeks or you can can it, using the Boiling Water Method that follows, and it will be shelf-stable for up to a year.
- To can your jelly using the Boiling Water Method, ladle it into clean, hot half-pint canning jars, leaving ¼ inch of headspace. Release any trapped air by swirling a clean chopstick or wooden skewer along the inside of the jar. Wipe the rims clean. Place the lids on top and screw the canning jar bands on just fingertip tight—that is just until the rings meet resistance when twisted on using only your fingertips.
- Use canning tongs to submerge the jars in boiling water to cover by 2 inches in a canner or pot fitted with a false bottom and cover with a lid. Process by boiling for 10 minutes. Turn off the heat and allow the jars to rest for 5 minutes. Use canning tongs to transfer the jars from the boiling water to a towel-covered surface. Allow to cool for 24 hours. Test the seals by removing the ring and gently but firmly pushing upward on the jar lid. If the seal is secure, store the jelly in a cool, dark place for up to a year. If the seal has failed, store the jelly in the refrigerator for up to 3 weeks.

Apple Tea

Fruit-flavored teas can be a great treat on a cool day or a lively refresher over ice. Many commercial fruit teas, however, are flavored artificially. You can make your own fruit-flavored tea with all the taste and none of the additives. This recipe is for apple tea, but you can use the same method for other fruits, such as pear, as well.

Makes 1 quart tea

5 teaspoons black tea, or 2 tea bags

1 to 2 cups apple peels (from 2 to 4 apples)

Granulated sugar

➡ Bring 1 quart of water to a boil. Add the tea leaves, encased in a tea ball, or the tea bags, and steep for 5 minutes. Remove the tea leaves and add the peels. Return the tea to a simmer, then turn off the heat. Allow the peels to steep until the tea has cooled completely. Strain the tea and compost or discard the peels. Serve over ice or reheat, sweetened with sugar, if desired. Keeps, refrigerated, for up to 5 days.

Apple Cordial

This little tipple is a terrific way to use up your apple peels. You can make up a batch anytime, but I think it tastes best on a chilly night, when you're curled up and cozy. You might consider making extra for friends—homemade hooch is a charming hostess gift.

You don't need any special equipment, just a good glass jar or bottle for storage. You can use the same infusion technique for any flavored booze or vinegar. Substitute berries, citrus peels, or spices such as vanilla beans, for delicious alternatives.

Makes up to 750 ml cordial

Peels from 3 to 4 apples (about 2 cups)

Up to 750 ml high-alcohol spirit (you can use whatever you like; vodka, rum,
   and whiskey are all great here, as long as it is 80 proof or more)

Up to 1 cup granulated sugar

Cider spices, such as a cinnamon stick, a couple of cloves,
   or a couple of coins of raw ginger (optional)

➡ Sterilize a glass jar that is big enough to hold the amount of peels you'll be infusing, by submerging it and its lid in boiling water for 10 minutes. Canning jars are great at handling that kind of heat, so they are a good option, but you can use any kind of jar you have on hand. Pack the peels into the sterilized jar. Cover completely with your spirit of choice. Add the sugar and any spices, if using. Screw the lid on the jar and shake. Place the jar in a cool, dark place for 1 to 2 weeks, shaking every day or so to distribute the flavors. Strain out the peels and spices, compost or discard them, and decant the liquid into another sterilized jar. Enjoy neat or on the rocks. The cordial keeps, in a cool, dark place, for up to 1 year.

Asparagus Stalks

There's a certain preciousness to asparagus. It has long been considered a treat—in ancient times it was considered a delicacy and prized for its supposed aphrodisiacal properties. Perhaps it's the vegetable's relative scarcity—it's a rare, fleeting thing in the market, having such a short season. Maybe it's the vegetable's architectural shape—so tall and stately—that makes it look so prim and proper. For these reasons and more, asparagus earns a little respect.

Buying: For best flavor and texture, look for bright, tight specimens. The tips should be well formed and still closed—not splaying open like a frayed bit of rope. The stalk should be firm with no signs of withering or drying. Asparagus that has been well cared for since it left the field will have smooth, moist ends that show no sign of drying or cracking.

Asparagus is often displayed for sale in a shallow pan of water. The water keeps the stalks from drying out and losing texture, which they would do very quickly without being able to sip away—asparagus is very thirsty. Make sure the water that holds them is clean and fresh. Lift up the asparagus bundle and have a peak at the bottoms of the stalks—they should look newly cut.

Storing: To get as much grassy goodness out of your lovely green or white shoots, it's important to store the vegetable properly so that it doesn't go all woody and tough before it hits the pan. Proper storage also means that you won't find yourself whittling away dry, spent asparagus along with your grocery dollars. When you get the asparagus home, "repot" them in a little fresh water. I like to put asparagus bundles in a nice big coffee mug, the weight of which makes tip-overs less likely. You can loosely drape a damp paper towel around the protruding tops. Put the whole setup in the fridge, where the asparagus will stay fresh for a day or two.

Prepping: Trim your asparagus right before you cook it. For a quick, rustic treatment, you can simply snap off the woody bottoms. To do it, grasp the stalk an inch or so from either end and bend away from you. The stalk will naturally snap where it starts to become woody. Alternatively, you can use a chef's knife to cut off the bottom of the stalks and use a vegetable peeler to peel off the tough outer skin from about 2 inches below the tip to the very bottom of the spear.

Save all trimmings and spears that are a bit past their prime to use in the recipes that follow. If you don't plan to use them right away, you can store your asparagus ends in an airtight container in the freezer and you'll always be just minutes away from that fresh, springtime flavor.

Asparagus Soup

I love this recipe for using up asparagus trimmings—it gives you all the flavor, but straining the soup leaves the tough texture of the peelings and woody ends behind. Super easy and elegant—a terrific "company's coming" throw-together.

Makes about 4 servings

2 tablespoons unsalted butter

1 shallot, diced, or 1 leek, white and light green parts diced
    (dark green stalks reserved for stock, page 107)

1 pound starchy potatoes, such as russets, peeled and chopped (about 2)
    (see page 84 for ways to use up potato peels)

2 cups asparagus trimmings

1 quart Blonde Chicken Stock (page 142) or Basic Vegetable Stock (page 107)

¼ cup heavy cream (optional but divine)

Salt and freshly ground black pepper

A few minced chives, croutons, or a little sour cream, for garnish (optional)

➡ Sauté the shallot or leek in the butter in a medium-size saucepan over medium heat until translucent, 3 to 5 minutes. Add the potatoes, asparagus trimmings, and stock and bring to a simmer. Cook until the potatoes are falling apart, about 25 minutes. Remove from the heat. Use an immersion blender to puree the soup. Alternatively, you can ladle the soup into a regular blender to puree (it's always a good idea to cover the blender with a tea towel and hold the lid down firmly to prevent potential volcanic action).

➡ Pour the blended soup through a fine-mesh strainer into a medium-size heatproof bowl, taking care to press as much of the thick asparagus pulp through the strainer as possible, leaving only the stringy, fibrous material behind. Return the strained soup to the pot and heat at a gentle simmer. If using the cream, add it and continue to simmer for 2 to 3 minutes. Adjust the seasoning with salt and pepper. Ladle into bowls and garnish, if you like, with chives, croutons, or sour cream.

➡ The soup (without the cream) can be cooled and refrigerated for 2 to 3 days or frozen for up to 3 months. Reheat and add the cream, if using, before serving.

Asparagus Butter

Keep this compound butter in the freezer to dress up a pot of white rice, a simple pasta dish, or a piece of broiled fish. Many compound butters are just softened butter into which various flavorings—often herbs or spices—have been incorporated. This butter also uses a little heated oil to bring out the taste of our flavoring ingredients—in this case asparagus, garlic, and lemon.

Makes about ¾ cup butter

¼ cup olive oil

1 cup asparagus trimmings

1 garlic clove, sliced

Zest of 1 lemon

8 ounces (2 sticks) unsalted butter, softened

➡ Heat the oil in a small sauté pan over low heat. Add the asparagus trimmings and simmer until softened, 8 to 10 minutes. Add the garlic and lemon zest and simmer until fragrant, about another minute. Remove from the heat. Puree the mixture in a small food processor, mortar and pestle, or the blending cup of an immersion blender. Press through a fine-mesh strainer to remove the solids. Allow to cool to room temperature. Combine the cooled oil and butter in a medium-size bowl and mash with a fork to blend completely. The butter will be a soft spread at room temperature but will firm when chilled. Cover and refrigerate for at least 2 hours and up to 5 days.

➡ The chilled butter can also be frozen. Lay a 12-inch length of plastic wrap or waxed paper on the counter. Transfer the butter mixture onto the wrap. Fold the wrap over the butter, pressing it into a log. Wrap the log in aluminum foil and freeze for up to 6 months. To use the butter, unwrap from the foil and slice off coins.

Asparagus Flan with Parsley Oil

This dish is an elegant starter for any meal. Its texture is light and lovely enough to kick off lunch, but the cream gives it a luxurious beginning to a sumptuous, even celebratory dinner.

This recipe calls for quite a few asparagus ends. You can accumulate this amount by saving the ends in a freezer-safe container as they become available throughout the season. Or you can use a combination of ends and stalks, if you find yourself with an abundance of spears and a shortage of patience.

Makes 6 servings

3 tablespoons unsalted butter, softened

3 cups asparagus ends

¼ cup heavy cream

3 large eggs

1 ounce Parmigiano-Reggiano cheese, grated (about ¼ cup)

Freshly ground black pepper

2 tablespoons parsley oil, for garnish (page 82) (optional)

➡ Preheat the oven to 350°F.

➡ Using 1 tablespoon of the butter, butter six ramekins, line the bottom of each with a circle of parchment paper, and butter the paper. Arrange the ramekins in a roasting pan large enough to hold them with at least 2 inches of space around each dish. Set aside.

➡ Steam the asparagus ends until very tender, 8 to 10 minutes. Combine the steamed asparagus, cream, and remaining 2 tablespoons of the butter and puree until smooth. Strain through a fine-mesh sieve into a medium-size heatproof bowl, taking the time to press out all the solids. Whisk in the eggs one at a time, blending completely after each addition. Whisk in the cheese and a few grinds of the pepper.

➡ Divide the mixture equally among the prepared ramekins. Add boiling water to the roaster to reach halfway up the sides of the ramekins. Bake until a tester inserted into the center of a flan comes out clean, 30 to 35 minutes. Let cool for 5 minutes.

➡ Run a sharp knife around the inside of a ramekin. Place a serving dish over the top and, holding the ramekin in place with an oven mitt, quickly flip the ramekin and dish over to release the flan. Repeat with the remaining flans.

➡ Drizzle the flans with parsley oil, if using, and serve immediately.

Beet and Turnip Greens

Beet greens. Who knew? Well, everyone, I hope. I'm on a personal mission to get eaters to enjoy their beet greens instead of—gasp!—throwing them away. And turnip greens, too. We may buy these foods for their roots, but the greens are equally attention worthy. They are as tasty as any other sautéing green, such as the newly minted rock star, kale—so much so, that you should really consider the health and vibrancy of these greens as much as the roots when you are purchasing your beets and turnips, so you can be sure you enjoy the one-two punch of both terrific parts of the plant.

You can treat beet greens as you would Swiss chard in many recipes. Their tender texture and mild flavor blend easily into dishes and make them very versatile. Turnip greens are a smidge more bitter. You can use them in recipes where you would normally include Asian choys, broccoli raab, or other hardy greens. Both beet and turnip "bonus" greens also have enough flavor to stand alone and are delectable in dishes that highlight their unique taste and texture.

Buying: For best flavor and texture look for bunches that have greens as crisp and spunky as any other leafy green for which you would shop. They should show limited signs of yellowing, withering, or insect damage. Trim off any that exist. Limp greens can be revived by submerging them in a basin of ice water for 5 to 10 minutes.

Storing: You can cook your greens right away or store them, wrapped in a reusable plastic bag or some damp paper towels, in your crisper drawer for 2 to 3 days. You can also cook them up and use them later. Both beet and turnip greens benefit from a quick sauté in olive oil and garlic—just be sure to start the chopped stems in the pan first to give them a chance to soften, then add the chopped leaves. Once all is tender, you can store them in the fridge for a few days to use in omelets or other recipes or you can transfer the sautéed greens to an airtight container and freeze for up to three months.

Prepping: To use the greens, cut them about an inch from their root. Wash thoroughly and use the O method (described on page 53) to separate the stems from the leaves or run a sharp paring knife down both sides of the rib to separate it from the leaf.

Quinoa Salad with Roots and Greens

Cooking both the greens and roots in this recipe makes for a winning combination of textures and flavors from the whole plant. The cranberries' sweetness riffs on the candy flavors of the beets and the pepitas bring a neat little
crunch to the party. And if you've never steamed your quinoa after boiling it,
as described below, do give that trick a try. It makes the grains fluffy and light.

Makes 6 to 8 servings

1 cup uncooked quinoa

1 (1-pound) bunch of beets, with greens

¼ cup olive oil

Salt and freshly ground black pepper

¼ cup red wine vinegar

2 tablespoons soy sauce

½ cup dried cranberries

½ cup raw pepitas (shelled pumpkin seeds) (see pages 88–89 for more info)

2 ounces Parmigiano-Reggiano cheese, grated (about ½ cup) (optional)

➡ Preheat the oven to 400°F.

Prepare the Quinoa

➡ Bring a large pot of salted water to a boil. Add the quinoa and boil until tender
and the germ begins to unfurl (it will look as if the grains have tails), about
15 minutes. Drain the quinoa through a fine-mesh strainer, return it to the
pot, cover, and allow to steam for 5 minutes. Transfer the cooked quinoa
to a large, flat container, such as a baking dish, and allow to cool to room
temperature.

Prepare the Beets

➡ Cut roots away from leaves, leaving 1 inch of stem attached to the roots.
Scrub the roots with a stiff brush to remove all dirt. Wrap the roots individually in foil, place on a
cookie sheet, and roast until cooked through, about 40 minutes. Unwrap the beets and allow to
cool. When cool enough to handle, slip off and discard the skins. Cut the beets into ½-inch dice
and set aside.

> **CHIFFONADE**
> Chiffonade is a technique
> for cutting leafy foods,
> such as greens or basil,
> into slivers. It's easily done
> by stacking the leaves on
> top of each other like a
> deck of cards, rolling the
> pile into a cigar shape, and
> slicing crosswise into strips
> of your desired width.

➡ *continues*

QUINOA SALAD WITH ROOTS AND GREENS continued

➡ Wash the beet leaves and spin or pat them dry. Remove any thick stems from the leaves (those thicker than a swizzle stick) and dice them. Cut the leaves into ¼-inch chiffonade. Sauté the chopped stems in 2 tablespoons of the olive oil and a pinch of salt and pepper, over medium heat until tender, 3 to 5 minutes. Add the leaves and cook until tender, another 5 to 7 minutes. Remove from the heat.

Prepare the Salad

➡ In a large bowl, combine the cooked quinoa, roasted beets, beet greens, and remaining ingredients, including the remaining 2 tablespoons of olive oil, and toss to blend flavors.

➡ Serve within 2 hours or refrigerate, covered, for up to 2 days.

Pasta with Greens

This is my go-to meal when I don't have a meal to go to at the end of a busy day. You can use greens that have already been sautéed (page 25), or just give them a quick sizzle in the pan while the noodles are boiling. The recipe makes a terrific blank slate for using up small amounts of leftovers you might have on hand. You can toss in some cooked chicken, meat, seafood, or vegetables, if you have them at the ready, or throw in a can of white beans, as I've suggested here. Or just serve the Pasta with Greens as is. Either way, the end result is satisfying comfort food in a flash.

Note: Starting the garlic in a cold pan may seem like an odd step, but it's the best way to extract the flavor from the cloves.

Makes 4 servings

8 ounces pasta, any shape you like

2 tablespoons olive oil

2 garlic cloves, sliced

2 cups beet or turnip greens, from 1 bunch of beets or turnips, leaves separated from ribs
    and leaves chopped, ribs diced

Salt and freshly ground black pepper

➡ *continues*

PASTA WITH GREENS *continued*

1 (15-ounce) can white beans, drained and rinsed, or up to 2 cups cooked chicken,

    meat, seafood, or vegetables (optional)

2 ounces Parmigiano-Reggiano cheese, grated (about ½ cup)

Pinch of red pepper flakes

➡ Boil the pasta in a large pot of salted, boiling water, for 1 minute less than the time indicated on the box (the pasta should be al dente, with a tiny dot of resistance at its center). Drain, reserving 1 cup of the pasta water.

➡ While the pasta is boiling, place the oil and garlic in a large sauté pan over medium heat. Once the oil begins to heat and the garlic begins to sizzle, stir it for 30 to 60 seconds, until fragrant. If the garlic begins to brown, lower the heat immediately; scorched garlic is bitter. Add the diced ribs to the pan and sauté until tender, 2 to 3 minutes. Add the greens to the pan and toss to coat them with the garlic and oil. Sprinkle with salt and pepper, lower the heat to medium-low, and sauté until wilted, stirring occasionally. Add the beans, protein, or other vegetables, if using, and heat through, stirring occasionally.

➡ Add the cooked pasta and ½ cup of the reserved pasta water to the pan and simmer for 1 to 2 minutes, until the pasta is cooked through.

➡ Remove from the heat and stir in half of the grated cheese to create a light sauce, adding more pasta water if necessary to loosen the mixture. Add the pepper flakes, give a final stir, and adjust the seasoning. Divide among four serving bowls and top with the remaining cheese.

Greens and Goat Cheese Pizza

Call it a nifty shortcut or a sneaky cheat, but using a tortilla as a pizza crust makes this little homemade pie a snap. Whip it up for lunch or a light dinner, or cut it into squares and serve it as an afterschool snack or cocktail nibble. I use sautéed greens and goat cheese as the toppings here, but you can riff on the recipe with any combos that you like: traditional tomato/mozzarella, Swiss/mushroom, fig/blue cheese and on and on. You can also use any size tortilla you have on hand or even rectangular lavash, if that's what's in your fridge. You can scale the goat cheese spread up or down, depending on the size of the pizza. It's all good. Really good.

➡ *continues*

Makes one 12-inch pizza

1 tablespoon olive oil

1 garlic clove, sliced

2 cups beet or turnip greens, from 1 bunch of beets or turnips,
    leaves separated from ribs and leaves chopped, ribs diced

Salt and freshly ground black pepper

2 ounces cream cheese, softened

2 ounces goat cheese, softened

1 to 2 teaspoons milk

¼ teaspoon dried thyme (optional)

1 (12-inch) tortilla, lavash, or wrap

➡ Place the oil and garlic in a medium-size sauté pan and swirl to coat the bottom of the pan. Set over medium heat. The garlic will transfer its flavor to the oil as the pan warms. When the garlic begins to sizzle, but before it browns (2 to 3 minutes), add the diced ribs to the pan and sauté until tender, 2 to 3 minutes. Add the greens to the pan and toss to coat them with the garlic and oil. Sprinkle with salt and pepper, lower the heat to medium-low, and sauté until wilted, stirring occasionally. Remove from the pan and set aside to cool slightly.

➡ While the greens cool, combine the cheeses in a medium-size bowl, mashing with a fork to blend. Add 1 to 2 teaspoons of milk, as necessary, to thin to a spreadable consistency. Add the thyme, if using, and a pinch of salt and pepper and stir to combine.

➡ Spread one side of the tortilla with the cheese spread. Strew the greens on top. Transfer the topped tortilla to the pan used to sauté the greens and set over medium-low heat. Allow the pizza to cook until the tortilla is toasted and crisp, about 5 minutes.

➡ Remove from the pan, cut into serving pieces, and serve.

Broccoli and Cauliflower Leaves

The first time I saw a fully grown, straight-from-the-fields head of cauliflower, I didn't even recognize it. An armful of a plant with layers of frilly leaves—almost petal-like—surrounding the tightly bound hub of florets of the plant. The creamy head—the part you usually see in the grocery store—was nestled deep inside the center of the leaves, like a bud waiting to bloom. It's a striking plant that earns the "flower" in its name. If you shop in the farmers' market, this is often how you will find them—gorgeous in all their glory.

Broccoli grows in a similar way—a head of florets surrounded by long, frilly leaves. However, broccoli is harvested differently from cauliflower. Rather than taking the head and leaves all in one pass, it is possible to harvest broccoli in a "cut and come again" fashion. The farmer removes the largest broccoli crowns from the plant, leaving the leaves intact. Side shoots will continue to grow where the head was harvested, developing florets that provide a second, side harvest. At this time, the leaves can be taken as well. So, while you will often find broccoli leaves in the market, you will rarely find them surrounding the central crown.

Don't see much broccoli or cauliflower leaf around at the market? Ask your farmer. It's a bonus crop that usually gets turned under when the plant stops producing but, like garlic scapes, is starting to gain ground in the market as eaters come to understand its uses and great flavor. And that's good news because these leaves aren't just gorgeous, they taste terrific—very similar to other Brassicas, such as kale, that are grown for their greenery.

Buying: When you are shopping for broccoli and cauliflower leaves, you want them to be bright green and fresh looking, with a limited amount of burnt edges or yellowing. Take a peek at the cut ends and avoid any that are excessively woody or dried-out looking. Patches of damage can be trimmed away. Wilted greens can be refreshed by submerging them in a basin of ice water for 5 to 10 minutes.

Storing: To keep the leaves, wrap them loosely in damp paper towels and store in the crisper for 2 to 3 days.

Prepping: To prep cauliflower and broccoli leaves for cooking, use a sharp paring knife to cut out the central rib. Just lay each leaf flat on your cutting board and slice down either side of the stem to remove it. You'll have a nice stack of the de-ribbed leaves in no time. You can cook the ribs separately, as you would chard stems.

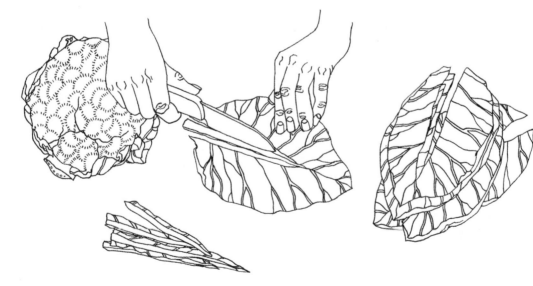

Roasted Brassica Leaves

Kale chips have become the belle of the ball in recent years. I predict the next gourmet chip will be these Roasted Brassica Leaves. Just like kale chips, they're a kid-friendly—and grown-up friendly—way to crisp up some greens into snackable bites. Serve these up and you, too, can be a hipster food trailblazer.

Makes 2 servings

1 bunch of broccoli or cauliflower leaves (7 to 10), ribs removed, chopped into 2-inch squares

2 tablespoons olive oil

Pinch of salt

➡ Preheat the oven to 350°F. Rub the leaf squares all over with the oil and arrange in a single layer on a cookie sheet. Sprinkle with salt. Bake until crisp and just starting to brown, 10 to 15 minutes. Remove from the oven, allow to cool, and serve immediately or store in an airtight container for up to a day.

Beef and Brassica Leaves

Beef and Broccoli is a popular Asian American dish. To get the most out of your broccoli, don't just include the florets. You can use all parts of the plant—the leaves, florets, and the stalks—in this recipe (see page 32 for more about trimming the stalks). Or you can use the leaves of the broccoli or cauliflower plants alone, as I've done here, to spotlight their unique flavor and texture.

Makes 4 to 6 servings

½ cup soy sauce

¼ cup rice vinegar or white wine vinegar

Pinch of granulated sugar

1½ pounds flank steak or skirt steak, cut into ¼-inch slices across the grain

1 cup chicken stock

➡ *continues*

BEEF AND BRASSICA LEAVES *continued*

Zest and juice of 1 orange

2 tablespoons cornstarch

3 tablespoons neutral oil, such as organic canola

1 onion, finely diced

2 garlic cloves, minced

1 (2-inch) piece ginger, finely minced

Leaves from 1 bunch of broccoli or cauliflower (7 to 10),
   ribs removed, leaves chopped into 2-inch pieces

1 teaspoon toasted sesame oil

➡ In a medium-size bowl, whisk the soy sauce, vinegar, and sugar until the sugar is dissolved. Pour half of the mixture into a small bowl and set it aside. Add the steak to the remaining mixture in the medium-size bowl and toss to coat. Allow to marinate for at least 15 minutes and up to an hour. Drain the steak and pat dry. Discard the used marinade.

➡ To the small bowl of reserved soy mixture, add the chicken stock, orange zest and juice, and cornstarch and whisk to blend. Set aside.

➡ Heat a large sauté pan over medium-high heat until a few drops of water dance when flicked on its surface. Add 1½ tablespoons of the neutral oil and the steak, spreading out the meat in an even layer. Allow the steak to brown well, 3 to 4 minutes, and then toss until browned all over but still pink in the center, another 2 to 3 minutes. Remove from the pan and set aside.

➡ Add the remaining 1½ tablespoons of the neutral oil and the onion and sauté until translucent and beginning to brown along the edges, about 5 minutes. Add the garlic and ginger and sauté until fragrant, 1 minute. Add the leaves and sauté until bright green, about 2 minutes. Add 2 tablespoons of water to the pan and cover. Allow the leaves to steam until tender, 3 to 5 minutes. Remove the lid from the pan, add the soy mixture, and bring to a boil to thicken the sauce. Return the steak to the pan and simmer for a minute or two to heat through. Serve immediately.

Brassica Leaf Colcannon

Colcannon is a traditional Irish side dish, popular on St. Patrick's Day, but deeply satisfying anytime, particularly when there's a chill in the air. Shredded cabbage is traditional, but it's a great recipe for using up brassica leaves as well. Kale is good, too. Cutting the leaves into chiffonade, thin strips (see page 27), ensures that they cook up nice and tender.

Makes 4 to 6 side dish servings

2 cups broccoli leaves, stems removed, cut into chiffonade

2 pounds starchy potatoes, such as russet, peeled and chopped (4 to 5 large)
   (see page 84 for ways to use up potato peels)

½ cup milk, warmed

¼ cup cold unsalted butter, cut into pats

Salt and freshly ground black pepper

→ Bring a large pot of salted water to a boil. Add the leaves, simmer for 1 minute, until tender. Remove with a slotted spoon, drain, and set aside. Add the potatoes and simmer until tender, 15 to 20 minutes. Drain the potatoes and return them to the pot. Add the milk and mash thoroughly with a potato masher or whip with an electric hand mixer until smooth. Add the butter in two parts, mashing or whipping after each addition. Fold in the blanched leaves. Season with salt and pepper and serve.

→ Keeps refrigerated for 2 to 3 days.

Broccoli Stalks

The stalks of the broccoli are my favorite. Many imagine them to be tough and fibrous, but they are actually quite the opposite. Once trimmed, the stalks are tender and sweet; they taste like a more delicate version of broccoli.

Buying: Of course, you want to walk right by the "broccoli crowns" often on offer at the market. These bunches of florets have already been robbed of their tender stalks. Instead, look for nice full heads of broccoli. Turn the bunch over and make sure that the bottom of the stalk looks relatively fresh, not overly woody, dried out, and split. If you are shopping in the farmers' market, you may just be lucky enough to get some broccoli leaves in the transaction as well. Visit page 31 to find out more about those.

Prepping: Julia Child was a fan of broccoli stalks, too, and it's her method for prepping them that I use today. Broccoli stalks are easy to trim: just cut off the florets and use a vegetable peeler to remove the tough outer layer of the stalk. Trim off the dry bottom. You can now cut the stalk into coins or batons or shred it on a box grater. That's all there is to it. Thanks, Julia!

Storing: If you need to store your stalks for a while, it's best to leave them untrimmed, wrapped in a damp paper towel or stored in an airtight container. They'll keep that way for 2 to 3 days.

Broccoli Slaw

If you are new to using broccoli stalks, this is a great "gateway" recipe. The tender stalks add just enough crunch and their delicate flavor really lets the Asian dressing shine. If you have extra veg on hand—some radishes, daikon, cabbage, peppers—you can prep them in the same manner and throw them in as well. This slaw is happy to play.

Makes 2 to 4 side dish servings

2 tablespoons soy sauce

1 tablespoon rice vinegar or white wine vinegar

Pinch of granulated sugar

1 teaspoon sesame oil

2 tablespoons neutral oil, such as organic canola

Red pepper flakes (optional)

Broccoli stalks from 1 bunch of broccoli, peeled, trimmed, and shredded or cut into matchsticks

2 carrots, shredded or cut into matchsticks

2 tablespoons minced fresh cilantro (optional)

2 tablespoons sesame seeds

➡ In a large bowl, whisk the soy sauce, vinegar, and sugar until the sugar is dissolved. Whisk in the oils and red pepper flakes, if using.

➡ Add the broccoli and carrots and toss to combine. Garnish with the cilantro, if using, and the sesame seeds. Can be made up to 2 hours ahead.

Chicken and Broccoli Stalk Stir-Fry

Chicken and Broccoli is an Asian American take-out standard. This recipe uses a light sherry sauce that is much more elegant, and much less goopy, than the standard brown sauce on many menus. The celery adds a really nice, aromatic flavor. On top of that, you can add any vegetables you have on hand.

Makes 6 to 8 servings

1 cup chicken stock (preferably homemade, see page 142)

2 tablespoons dry sherry

2 tablespoons soy sauce

1 tablespoon cornstarch

2 tablespoons neutral oil, such as organic canola

2 pounds chicken thighs, cut into 2-inch pieces

1 onion, diced

2 celery stalks, thinly sliced

Stalks from one bunch of broccoli, trimmed and cut into coins

1 cup assorted cooked vegetables, such as carrots cut into coins, spinach, or bok choy (optional)

1 (1-inch) piece fresh ginger, minced

1 garlic clove, minced

½ cup roasted cashews

➡ In a small bowl, whisk the stock, sherry, soy sauce, and cornstarch until well blended. Set aside.

➡ Heat a large sauté pan over medium-high heat until a few drops of water dance when flicked on its surface. Add the oil and swirl to coat the pan. Add the chicken and sauté until browned, but not cooked through, 5 to 7 minutes. Push the chicken to the sides of the pan and add the onion, celery, and broccoli stalks to the center. Sauté until the onion is translucent, about 5 minutes. Add the cooked vegetables, if using, and stir to combine everything in the pan. Add the ginger and garlic and sauté until fragrant, about 1 minute. Add the stock mixture and bring to a boil to thicken. Lower the heat, cover, and simmer until the chicken is cooked through, 5 minutes more. Remove from the heat, top with the cashews, and serve.

Broccoli and Cheddar Soup

A combination of stems and florets work best in this soup—you need the assertive flavor of the florets to stand up against the cheese. But using the stems balances out the flavor (and your budget), so why not?

Makes 4 servings

1 quart chicken or vegetable stock (preferably homemade, see pages 142 and 107)

1 bunch of broccoli (1½ to 2 pounds), florets separated from stems and stems peeled, trimmed, and chopped (see page 36)

4 tablespoons unsalted butter

2 garlic cloves, minced

¼ cup all-purpose flour

½ cup heavy cream

6 ounces sharp Cheddar cheese, grated (about 1½ cups)

Salt and freshly ground black pepper

Several fresh gratings of nutmeg (reserve the rest of the nutmeg seed for another use)

➡ Bring the stock to a boil in a medium-size saucepan. Add the broccoli stems and simmer for 1 to 2 minutes. Add the broccoli florets and continue to simmer until all the broccoli is tender, about 5 minutes. Remove from the heat and puree with an immersion blender or in a standard blender, being careful not to splash yourself with the hot liquid. Set aside the puree.

➡ In a large, heavy saucepan over medium heat, sauté the garlic in the butter until fragrant, about 1 minute. Add the flour and sauté until the flour just begins to color, 2 to 3 minutes. Slowly add the broccoli puree, whisking constantly, until smooth. Add the cream and return the heat to a simmer. Remove from the heat and add the cheese, one handful at a time, whisking after each addition until smooth. Season with salt and pepper and nutmeg. Divide among four bowls and serve. The soup keeps, cooled, covered, and refrigerated, for up to 2 days. Reheat before serving..

Brussels Sprout Leaves

If you buy your Brussels sprouts in the grocery store, you are probably used to seeing them on offer as a small tub of what look like tiny cabbages. In the farmers' market they are sometimes offered on the stalk, which looks like a large baton covered with the tiny cabbages. But if you were to see them in the field, Brussels sprouts are actually a rather leafy thing. Tall and imposing, the stalk grows straight up, the sprouts dotting it sides and, interspersed between the sprouts are wide leaves that branch out in all directions. It looks more like a bush than you might imagine.

All parts of the plant are edible—at least, the "above the ground" part. The sprouts are the most commonly enjoyed part of the plant, of course. Even the towering stalk, which needs to be hacked into 6-inch sections first, can then be steamed or braised until tender to get to the creamy, pulpy, marrowlike center. But it's those big leaves—the ones that fan out from the stalk—that I am cooking in these recipes. The leaves are delicious and easy to work with and tragically neglected, in my view.

Buying: When shopping for Brussels sprout leaves, like any other leaves, you want them to be bright green and lively looking. Trim away spots of yellowing or insect damage. Wilted leaves can be refreshed by submerging them in a basin of ice water for 5 to 10 minutes.

Storing: Brussels sprout leaves keep, wrapped in damp paper towels or an airtight container and refrigerated, for 2 to 3 days.

Prepping: Brussels sprout leaves are very similar in taste and texture to collard greens and can be substituted in recipes that call for them. If the leaves are very large and the ribs tough, you can strip the leaves as you would those of any other leafy green, either by cutting the rib out with sharp paring knife or using the O method (page 53). You can use the ribs as well; just dice them and add to the pot several minutes ahead of the leaf, to give them a jump on tenderizing.

Sprout Leaves with Bacon

Bacon makes it better, it's true. The rich flavor of the meat pairs so beautifully with the funky, slightly bitter taste of the Brassicas—broccoli, cauliflower, Brussels sprouts, and cabbage all benefit from a date with the stuff. If you are new to Brussels sprout leaves, start with this recipe—it's a crowd-pleaser.

Makes 4 servings

¼ pound bacon, diced (about 4 strips)

1 small onion, diced

Salt

6 to 8 Brussels sprout leaves, ribs removed, if necessary, and leaves cut into 2-inch pieces

Freshly ground black pepper

➡ Sauté the bacon in a medium-size skillet over medium-low heat until the fat has rendered out and the bacon is brown and crisp. Use a slotted spoon to remove the bacon from the pan and drain on paper towels or a brown paper bag. Raise the heat to medium and sauté the onion, sprinkled with a little salt, until translucent, 3 to 5 minutes. Add the leaves to the pan and sauté until bright green and wilted, 2 to 3 minutes. Add 2 tablespoons of water to the pan and cover. Steam the leaves until tender, about 5 minutes. Remove the lid from the pan and continue to simmer until all moisture is evaporated. Return the cooked bacon to the pan and stir to heat through. Season with salt and pepper and serve.

➡ Will keep, cooled, covered, and refrigerated, for 2 to 3 days.

Stuffed Sprout Leaves

My father's side of the family is Polish and I grew up eating terrific Eastern European dishes prepared by my Granny Toni, my grandmother, and my great-aunts. My southern mother even adopted a few of these soul-satisfying and budget-stretching recipes. One that she turned out most often was galumpki—a big casserole of cabbage rolls stuffed with meat and rice and napped in a tangy tomato sauce. Here, I use a similar recipe, substituting sprout leaves for the cabbage. The trick to rolling the wrappers without tearing them is to blanch the leaves first.

Makes 6 servings

2 tablespoons olive oil

2 onions, diced

4 garlic cloves, minced

32 ounces whole tomatoes, preferably home-canned, pureed with their juices

1 teaspoon light or dark brown sugar

12 Brussels sprout leaves

2 pounds ground beef, preferably grass-fed

2 large eggs

2 cups cooked white rice

1 teaspoon ground allspice

➡ Sauté half of the diced onions in a medium-size skillet until translucent, 3 to 5 minutes. Add half of the garlic and sauté until fragrant, about 1 minute. Add the tomatoes and brown sugar and bring to a boil. Lower the heat to low and simmer until thickened, about 15 minutes. Remove from the heat.

➡ Meanwhile, bring a large pot of water to a boil. Prep a large bowl of ice water and set aside. Add the leaves, six at a time, to the boiling water and blanch for 30 seconds. Use a slotted spoon to remove the leaves from the boiling water and immediately plunge into the ice water to stop the cooking. Repeat with the remaining leaves. Set aside.

➡ In a large bowl, use your hands to combine the rest of the onion and garlic, meat, eggs, rice, allspice, and ½ cup of the tomato sauce to be the filling.

➡ Spread ½ cup of the sauce in the bottom of an 11 by 17-inch casserole. Assemble the rolls by placing 2 tablespoons of filling over the bottom third of a leaf. Fold the sides up over the filling and then roll away from you to encase the filling. Place the roll, seam side down, in the casserole. Repeat with

➡ continues

the remaining leaves. Pour the remaining sauce over the rolls. Bake, uncovered, until the internal temperature of the rolls reaches 165°F, about an hour. Serve with sour cream and a nice cold beer.

➡ The cooked casserole keeps cooled, covered, and refrigerated for up to 3 days, and in the freezer for up to 3 months.

Sprout Leaf Salad with Couscous and Roasted Butternut Squash

Here, the leaves are "cooked" in the dressing to tenderize them—a trick that also works as a treat with raw kale. It's important to shred the leaves in a fine chiffonade (see page 27) to get the right texture—if the leaves are too big, they won't wilt under the acidity of the dressing and they'll be too chewy to enjoy. The squash brings a sweetness to the dish that plays off the tang of the dressing and, with the couscous, makes this salad a satisfying meal.

Makes 4 servings

6 Brussels sprout leaves, ribs removed, if necessary, and leaves cut into ¼-inch chiffonade

¼ cup red wine vinegar

1 shallot, diced

1 pound butternut squash, peeled, seeded, and cut into 1½-inch cubes

¼ cup plus 1 tablespoon olive oil

1 cup Israeli or pearl couscous

2 ounces pecorino cheese, grated (about ½ cup)

Salt and freshly ground black pepper

➡ Preheat the oven to 400°F.

➡ In a large bowl, toss the leaves with the vinegar and shallot and set aside to "cook."

➡ Meanwhile, prepare the rest of the salad: Toss the squash with 1 tablespoon of the olive oil and roast until tender, about 20 minutes. While the squash is roasting, boil the couscous in medium-size pot of salted water until tender, 10 to 12 minutes. Drain and set aside.

➡ To assemble the salad, toss the leaf mixture with the couscous. Let rest for a few minutes to allow the pasta to absorb some of the vinegar. Add the remaining ¼ cup of olive oil and toss again. Add the cheese and stir to combine. Gently fold in the cooled squash. Season with salt and pepper and serve.

➡ The salad keeps, cooled, covered, and refrigerated, for 2 to 3 days.

Carrot Tops

Can you really eat those? I get that question whenever I serve carrot fronds. Surprising as it may seem—yes, you can. And you should. Perhaps because we are so used to sending them directly to the bin, it's hard to picture the fluff of green fronds as anything edible. There have been rumors, too, that carrot tops are poisonous. And many eaters must believe it—shopping at the farmers' market, growers often ask whether I would like the tops removed for easier transport. And give away these sprightly green sprigs? No way. Not only are carrot tops perfectly safe, they are loaded with the same fantastic nutrients that make other green vegetables so attractive.

Buying: The bonus of buying carrots with their fronds attached is that the greens are a sure sign of freshness. Old carrots cannot have fresh fronds. Look for carrot fronds that are dark green and fluffy with no sign of wilting. Old fronds that are beginning to fade will lose their loft and start to sag and look heavy. At the end of their life, carrot fronds will turn black and slimy— time for the compost.

Storing: Carrots are keepers and, like all root vegetables, will long outlast their greens. You can store the carrot roots (the orange part in your typical carrot) wrapped in damp paper towels or plastic in the refrigerator for a week or more, or in a bucket of damp sand in your root cellar, if that's how you roll. The greens, on the other hand, will only keep for a brief stay in the fridge— once separated from their roots, you can get one to two days out of them if they are wrapped in plastic or a damp paper towel.

Prepping: Carrot fronds can be a touch bitter—in that sophisticated broccoli raab way. Nip off a pinch of frond and give it a taste. Most young roots have mild greens that can go right into your recipe. If you find the taste too strong, you can blanch them by quickly dropping them in a pot of boiling water and then shocking the greens in some ice water to remove some of the bitter flavor.

I like to make sure carrot fronds are paired with ingredients that balance their bite. A good glug of olive oil or other rich counterpart; something sweet, like the carrot roots themselves; or tangy, like citrus, ensures that the edginess of the greens doesn't dominate. So, put those carrot greens to work—your friends will be amazed and your taste buds will be, too.

Carrot Top Gremolata

Gremolata, an Italian herb and citrus garnish, is one of those little tricks that turn a nice home cooked meal into a white tablecloth experience. No joke. Sprinkle a little on top of some braised pot roast, a bowl of stew, or some richly caramelized roasted vegetables and gremolata's bright blast of flavor will take your dish to the next level. And it's so easy to make.

Makes about ¼ cup gremolata

1 garlic clove

Zest of 1 lemon

¼ cup carrot fronds

½ teaspoon kosher salt

- Cut the garlic clove in half. Lay half of the clove, flat side down, on a cutting board and rest the heel of a large knife on top of the clove. Strike the knife with the heel of your hand to smash the clove half. Repeat with the other clove half.
- Make a pile of the lemon zest, smashed garlic, and carrot fronds in the center of your cutting board. Sprinkle the pile with the salt. Finely mince the ingredients, using a rocking motion with the edge of your knife against the cutting board to slice through the pile rather than crush it. Stop occasionally to wipe the sides of the blade over the pile. Continue mincing until all the ingredients are pulverized. Use within an hour or so, or the gremolata will begin to weep.

Whole Carrot Soup

This soup uses both the roots and the tops of the carrots. The carrot tops bring a beautiful swirl of color to your bowl—gorgeous autumnal tones for the fall table. Their bitter flavor really nudges up wonderfully next to the dish's sweetness. You can make both components ahead for easy entertaining.

Makes 4 to 6 servings

1 pound carrots, fronds removed from roots and set aside, roots peeled and roughly chopped

2 tablespoons freshly squeezed lemon juice

¼ cup plus 2 tablespoons olive oil

Salt and freshly ground black pepper

1 small onion, diced

1 pound russet potatoes, peeled (about 2 large) (see page 84 for ways to use up potato peels)

1 quart chicken or vegetable stock (for homemade, see pages 142 and 107), or water

➡ Puree ½ cup of the carrot fronds and the lemon juice, ¼ cup of the olive oil, and a pinch of salt and pepper in a small food processor, blender, or with an immersion blender. Set aside.

➡ Sauté the onion in a medium-size saucepan over medium heat in the remaining 2 tablespoons of olive oil until translucent, 3 to 5 minutes. Add the carrot roots, potatoes, and stock and bring to a boil. Lower the heat and simmer for 20 to 25 minutes, or until extremely tender. Puree the soup in a blender or with an immersion blender, being careful not to splash yourself with the hot liquid. Season to taste.

➡ Divide the soup among four bowls and drizzle a swirl of the frond mixture on top. Serve immediately.

➡ The soup and frond drizzle keep, cooled, covered, and refrigerated, for 2 to 3 days, or frozen for up to 3 months.

Carrot Top Pesto

The trick to using carrot fronds in pesto is to counterbalance the bitterness of the greens. I've found the best way to do this is to use a really buttery nut, such as cashews or macadamias, to even out the taste of the sauce. Using a neutral-flavored oil, such as organic canola, also cuts down on the bite a bit.

Use this pesto to top crostini for a little nibble, as a dip for crudités, or a sauce for pasta. It also freezes really well, so feel free to double the batch and store some away for later.

Makes about 1½ cups pesto

½ cup unsalted, roasted cashews

½ cup loosely packed carrot fronds

1 garlic clove

4 ounces Parmigiano-Reggiano cheese, grated (about 1 cup)

1 cup organic canola oil

Juice and zest of 1 lemon

Salt and freshly ground black pepper

➡ Combine all the ingredients in a blender and puree until smooth. Adjust the seasoning. Thin with a little water, if necessary. Serve immediately, cover and refrigerate for 2 to 3 days, or freeze in an airtight container for up to 6 months.

Celery Leaves

Celery leaves should be classified as an herb. They are deeply flavorful and bring a bright, aromatic touch to the table. Unlike other fronds, which taste fresh and grassy, celery leaves have a taste that is much more complex than "green." It's more like a cross between the stalks and a bitter lettuce. They play well with other flavors, too—from subtle shellfish to funky blue cheese. I especially love to substitute celery leaves for flat-leaf parsley when it's called for in a recipe; it creates a more complex, yet still herbal flavor.

Buying: If you are shopping in the farmers' market, it's easy to find heads of celery topped abundantly with frilly bouquets of leaves. Supermarkets often trim away many of the leaves, but you can still find a fair amount on full heads of celery. Celery hearts, on the other hand, have had all but the inner stalks and leaves cut away, so you will be missing out on this leafy treat if you select those.

Storing: The leaves stay fresh and nice for quite a while. Just wrap the whole head loosely in a reusable plastic bag or in some damp paper towels and tuck it away in your crisper drawer, where it will keep crunchy and bright for at least two and up to three weeks before it starts to go sad and limp. When this happens you can resuscitate the veg by separating the stalks and plunging them into a bowl of ice water. After a few hours, the celery will revive and be crisp and ready again, giving you an extra 3 to 4 days before it begins to slip toward compost heaven.

Prepping: When you are ready to enjoy your celery leaves, just pinch or snip them off the stalks. You can use them whole in salads or mince them as you would parsley.

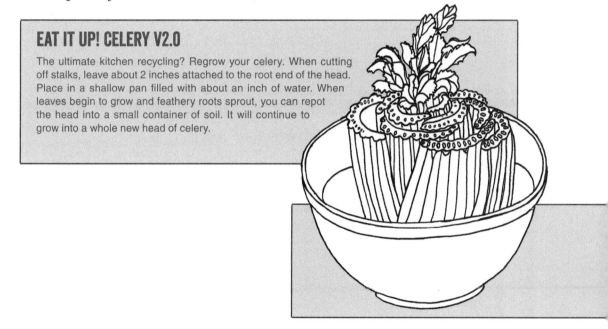

EAT IT UP! CELERY V2.0

The ultimate kitchen recycling? Regrow your celery. When cutting off stalks, leave about 2 inches attached to the root end of the head. Place in a shallow pan filled with about an inch of water. When leaves begin to grow and feathery roots sprout, you can repot the head into a small container of soil. It will continue to grow into a whole new head of celery.

Celery and Radish Salad

Sprightly is the word that comes to mind when I think of this salad. The tastes really leap out at you—tangy dressing, aromatic greens, and a little heat from the radish. Use the tender, inner leaves for this salad, rather than the dark green leaves from the outer stalks, which would overpower. It's bold enough to garnish a juicy steak, and I can't think of anything with which it would be better paired. (And for more on radish leaves, see pages 94–97.)

Makes 4 servings

1 teaspoon Dijon mustard

1 tablespoon white wine vinegar

Salt and freshly ground black pepper

¼ cup neutral oil, such as organic canola

4 stalks celery with leaves, stalks cut into ¼-inch slices, leaves left whole

4 radishes with leaves, roots thinly sliced, leaves cut into chiffonade

2 ounces good blue cheese, such as Bayley Hazen Blue, crumbled

→ In a medium-size bowl, whisk together the mustard, vinegar, and a pinch each of salt and pepper until the salt dissolves. Gradually add the oil in a steady stream, whisking all the while to emulsify.

→ Add the celery and radishes with their prepped leaves and toss with the vinaigrette. Divide among four plates and top with the cheese. Serve immediately.

Celery Leaf Fattoush

This riff on the Middle Eastern pita bread salad uses celery leaves instead of flat-leaf parsley and puts stale pita to good use, too—double happiness. It's a salad that begs for additions so feel free to throw in any extras that appeal— some cooked veg or meat, chicken, or fish, a few beans, or some nice, tangy cheese, such as feta or goat, would make this salad a meal.

Makes 4 servings

1 (9-inch) or 2 (4-inch) stale pita breads

¼ cup plus 1 tablespoon olive oil

Zest and juice of 1 lemon (about ¼ cup)

Salt and freshly ground black pepper

2 tomatoes, seeds removed, chopped

1 English cucumber or 2 Persian cucumbers, seeded and diced

1 small red onion or shallot, diced, rinsed under cold water, and drained

1 cup celery leaves, chopped

¾ cup fresh mint, minced

2 cups chopped lettuce, such as iceberg or romaine

2 cups meal-maker additions, such as cooked veg or meat, chicken, or fish,
    cooked beans, or feta or goat cheese (optional)

➡ Chop or break the bread into bite-size pieces. Over medium heat, toast the pita in a medium-size sauté pan that has been coated with 1 tablespoon of the olive oil. Set aside.

➡ In a small bowl, whisk together the remaining ¼ cup of olive oil, lemon zest and juice, and a pinch of salt and pepper. Set aside.

➡ In a large bowl, combine the toasted pita pieces and remaining ingredients. Toss with the dressing, adjust the seasoning, and set aside for 5 to 10 minutes to allow the flavors to combine. Toss again and serve.

➡ Can be made up to 2 hours ahead and refrigerated.

Rice Pilaf

Rice pilaf sounds so 1950s, I love it! Very old school. But, frankly, I don't know how it ever went out of style. It's tasty and versatile and offers an easy twist on a pot of plain white rice. And, bonus, kids seem to gobble it up. I use chicken stock here, but you can use vegetable stock or water if you want to keep it meat-free. Sautéing the rice in the olive oil keeps the grains separate so the pilaf stays nice and fluffy. The saffron brings a vibrant color and a subtle, exotic flavor. If you don't have it on hand, you can substitute ½ teaspoon of ground turmeric.

Makes 4 servings

1 cup long-grain white rice

2 tablespoons olive oil

1 small onion, diced

1 carrot, peeled and diced

1 celery stalk, cut into ¼-inch slices

Salt and freshly ground black pepper

1 garlic clove, minced

½ cup celery leaves, chopped

½ cup white wine

2 cups chicken or vegetable stock (for homemade, see pages 142 and 107), or water

Pinch of dried thyme

Pinch of saffron threads

¼ cup slivered almonds (optional)

➡ Sauté the rice in the olive oil in a medium-size saucepan over medium heat for 1 to 2 minutes. Add the onion, carrot, and celery and a pinch of salt and pepper and sauté until the onion is translucent, 3 to 5 minutes. Add the garlic and celery leaves and sauté until fragrant, about 1 minute.

➡ Add the wine, stock, thyme, and saffron and cover. Bring to a boil. Stir once and cover. Lower the heat to its lowest level and gently simmer for 15 minutes. Remove from the heat and set aside for 10 minutes to steam (do not lift the lid!). Fluff the rice and transfer to a serving dish. Top with the slivered almonds, if you like.

Chard, Kale, and Collard Stems

While it's true that we often strip out the stems from leafy greens, such as chard, kale, and collards, before proceeding with many recipes, that doesn't mean that they have to be tossed. Oftentimes, you can add them to the same dish by starting them in the pot first to give them a chance to soften before adding the quick cooking leaves. Or you can cook the stems separately in their own dish to highlight their unique texture. Some stems, such as those from collard greens, are great raw.

Buying: To get good stems, look for good leaves—bright and fresh. The stems should have enough life in them to snap when broken. A bit of insect damage or rot can be trimmed away. Wilted leaves can be refreshed by submerging in a basin of ice water for 5 to 10 minutes.

Prepping: I use two methods for removing stems from all my leafy greens. For soft-leaved greens, such as Swiss chard, turnip and beet greens, and kale, I use the O method. To do it, grab a leaf by the stem in your nondominant hand. Cuff the thumb and first finger around the bottom of the leaf just where it meets the stem, making an O with your two fingers. Firmly and quickly, pull the leaf through the O. The stem will tear away as you pull, separating the two parts of the plant. For sturdier leaves, such as collards, I cut the stem out. Simply lay your leaf flat on the cutting board and, with a paring knife, slice down both sides of the stem to remove it.

Storing: If you are not going to cook your stems immediately, you can wrap them in reusable plastic bags or damp paper towels and store them in your crisper drawer for 2 to 3 days.

Caldo Verde (Portuguese Kale Soup)

This soul-warming soup is a Portuguese staple. The potatoes thicken the base, so it's nice and hardy—a real rib-sticker. I've added sausage here—as many recipes do—but you could leave it out and sub in vegetable stock for a vegetarian version. Be sure to cut your kale into fine ribbons for the best texture.

Makes 4 servings

½ pound Portuguese chouriço, linguiça, or smoked kielbasa, cut into ¼-inch coins

2 tablespoons olive oil

1 bunch of kale, stems removed and diced, leaves cut into ⅛-inch chiffonade

1 onion, diced

2 garlic cloves, sliced

1½ pounds waxy potatoes, such as fingerlings, peeled and chopped (see page 84 for ways to use
   up potato peels)

2 quarts Blonde Chicken Stock (page 142), Basic Vegetable Stock (page 107), or water

Salt and freshly ground black pepper

➡ In a Dutch oven or other heavy-bottomed pot, sauté the sausage in the oil over medium heat until it begins to brown around the edges. Add the diced kale stems and onion and sauté until the onion is translucent, 3 to 5 minutes. Add the garlic and sauté until fragrant, about 1 minute. Add the potatoes and stock and bring to a boil. Lower the heat and simmer until the potatoes are nearly tender, about 15 minutes. Add the shredded kale leaves and simmer until they're tender but still have some texture, about 5 minutes. Season with salt and pepper and serve.

➡ The soup keeps, cooled, covered, and refrigerated, for 2 to 3 days.

Stem Pickles

Pickles don't always have to equal *cucumbers*. Got chard stems? Use this quick refrigerator pickle to transform them into a tasty, tangy treat. Their texture, similar to that of celery, softens just enough in the brine to be pleasing but still retains its crunch. Use rainbow chard for a more colorful concoction.

Makes 2 cups pickles

2 cups chard stems, cut ½ inch shorter than the height of your jar

1 cup cider vinegar

2 tablespoons granulated sugar

2 teaspoons salt

1 teaspoon mustard seeds

½ teaspoon chili flakes

➡ Pack the stems vertically into a 1-pint canning jar. In a small saucepan over high heat, combine remaining ingredients with ½ cup of water and bring to a boil. Stir for 1 to 2 minutes to dissolve the sugar and salt. Pour the brine over the stems. Swirl the jar to remove any air bubbles and top with more brine, if necessary, to completely cover the stems. Allow to cool to room temperature. Cover and refrigerate for at least 2 days and up to 3 weeks.

Stem Crostini

I once served this to a group of kids during a farm camp cooking session. Actually, they made it and then ate it, so maybe that was part of the appeal. Bottom line—they loved it. Even the greens haters. If you have littles that won't eat their greens, try this recipe. If you can get them to help with the prep, even better. This is also good with kale or turnip or beet greens.

Makes 24 crostini

2 tablespoons olive oil

1 small onion, diced

1 garlic clove, sliced

1 bunch of chard, kale, or beet or turnip greens, stems cut into ½-inch pieces,
   leaves sliced into chiffonade

½ cup chicken or vegetable stock (for homemade, see pages 142 and 107)

¼ cup raisins

2 ounces Parmigiano-Reggiano cheese, grated (about ½ cup)

Salt and freshly ground black pepper

24 crostini (see note)

➡ Sauté the onion in the olive oil in a medium-size sauté pan over medium heat until translucent, 3 to 5 minutes. Add the garlic and sauté until fragrant, about 1 minute. Add the greens stems and sauté until al dente, 2 to 3 minutes. Add the leaves and sauté until bright green, 2 to 3 minutes. Add the stock and raisins and cover the pan. Braise the greens for about 5 minutes, until they are tender and the raisins are plump. Remove from the heat and stir in the cheese. Season with salt and pepper. Top each crostini with the greens mixture and serve immediately.

★ **Note:** You can buy premade crostini, which are simply toasted baguette slices, but it's easy enough to make your own. To make crostini, cut a French baguette into ¼-inch diagonal slices. Drizzle with olive oil and broil until browned, 1 to 2 minutes. Use tongs to turn the crostini over and broil the other side an additional 1 to 2 minutes.

Citrus Peels

Citrus peels are magical. The citrus oil they contain makes them the most flavorful and aromatic part of the fruit, full of floral notes and heady fragrance not found in the juice. The zest—the thin, colored part of the peel—has intense citrus taste and is often a secret ingredient that I use in everything from salad dressings to baked goods. Even the pith, which can be wickedly bitter when used straight off the fruit, can be tamed into submission.

Buying: When buying citrus with the intent of using the peels, it's best to get unwaxed fruit, if you can find it, or to remove as much of the wax as you can before proceeding with your recipe. You also want to look for organic fruit or fruit grown using IPM (integrated pest management) methods when possible to avoid exposure to toxic residues.

Storing: Citrus fruits keep, refrigerated, for at least a week. If not using immediately, zest can be frozen or dried once it is removed from the fruit.

Prepping: Before jumping into any citrus recipe, whether you are going to use the zest or not, it's a good idea to wash the fruit thoroughly. That way you won't introduce surface contaminants into the fruit when you slice it. To remove wax from fruit, you can give it a scrub with warm water, a drop of fragrance-free dish soap, and a soft brush. Don't use water that is too hot or a brush that is too stiff or you will remove citrus oil and damage the skin of the fruit.

While some recipes, such as marmalade, use the whole rind, more often than not, you'll be asked for only citrus zest. There are two quick and easy ways to remove the zest. If you are looking for big pieces, perhaps to use in an infusion or dunk down into a braise, simply use a sharp vegetable peeler to remove them from the fruit. Adjust the pressure you use so that you don't remove too much of the pith with the strips of zest. If your strips are too pithy, simply lay them flat on a cutting board and use a sharp paring knife to scrape off the white pith until you have nothing but brightly colored zest.

The second method that I use for zesting is to employ a Microplane. You may have seen these in the hardware store or specialty kitchen store. It looks like a wood plane and produces tons of tiny shavings that disperse beautifully when blended into your recipes. To use the Microplane, lay it over a bowl, teeth side up. Grasp the plane with your nondominant hand. Firmly scrape the citrus over the cutting edge of the plane's teeth. Use only a single pass over the plane, turning the fruit so that a new section of skin is exposed each time you swipe, to avoid shredding into the bitter pith.

Citrus Extract

Most extracts on the market aren't really extracts at all. They are chemical-laden flavorings that get their taste from science, not nature. Well-made extracts can be hard to find and are mighty expensive when you do. But you have a homemade fix for that in this template of a recipe. I've used citrus here and you can use any kind—lemon, orange, lime, and more—or substitute other peels or spices, such as ginger trimmings, cinnamon sticks, or vanilla pods for an array of tasty extracts.

Makes 1 cup extract

½ cup citrus peels, white pith removed

1 cup not-your-best vodka

➡ Sterilize a pint-size canning jar by submerging it in boiling water for 10 minutes. Drain the jar and add the peels to it. Pour the vodka over the peels. Cover the jar and shake it. Set aside in a cool, dark place for 2 weeks, shaking the jar every few days. Remove the peels. Store in a cool, dark place and enjoy the extract in all your homemade recipes for up to 1 year.

Candied Peels

You can make these candied peels from many varieties of citrus—orange and grapefruit peels are particularly delicious. They look great when they're done and are often given as gifts, particularly around the holidays when citrus is in season and their sparkly sugar coating twinkles festively. Dip the ends in melted chocolate for a decadent touch.

Makes about 4 cups peel

Peels, including pith, from 2 well-scrubbed grapefruit

5 cups granulated sugar

1 vanilla bean

8 ounces dark chocolate, chopped (optional)

- Place a drying rack over a baking sheet and set aside.
- Cut the peels into ¼-inch strips. Cover the peels with cold water in a large nonreactive saucepan and bring to a boil. Strain and repeat two more times to remove the bitter flavor from the pith and to soften the peels. After the third boil, drain the peels and set aside while you make the syrup.
- Bring 2 cups of water to a boil and gradually add 4 cups of the sugar, stirring to dissolve. Add the peels and the vanilla bean. Return the heat to a boil, and then lower the heat to a simmer. Cook gently until the peels are translucent and tender, about 1 hour.
- Using tongs, transfer the peels to the prepared drying rack and separate them so they don't touch. Let drain, and dry for 4 to 5 hours or overnight. When quite dry but still tacky, roll the peels in the remaining 1 cup of sugar to coat. The peels keep, stored in an airtight container, for up to 1 month.
- If dipping the peels, melt the chocolate in a double boiler over low heat. Dip dried peels in the chocolate to cover halfway up the peel. Allow excess chocolate to drain, and place on a parchment-lined cookie sheet. Repeat with remaining peels. Allow to cool until chocolate solidifies, about an hour or so, before removing from the sheet.

Citrus and Chili Dust

This homemade seasoning is a great no-cook way to use up citrus rinds. You can use chilis that you have dried yourself or any commercially available chili. Smokey anchos (the smoked, dried version of poblano peppers) are my favorite here; they have more flavor than heat, making this mix all the more versatile. Use it in marinades and dressings, sprinkle it on meat, fish, and vegetables, or—my favorite—hot buttered popcorn.

Makes a scant ¼ cup dust

4 lemons or 2 oranges

1 ancho chili

➡ Using a vegetable peeler, remove the zest from the fruit in wide strips. Arrange the zest in a single layer on a wire rack. Set aside in a dry place with good air circulation, until it becomes brittle. Alternatively, you can dry it in a low oven, set to about 170°F.

➡ Use kitchen shears or a sharp knife to open up the chili. Pull away the stem and scrape out the seeds. Roughly chop the chili.

➡ Combine the dried zest and chili in a clean coffee grinder. Whir until pulverized. The seasoning keeps in an airtight container for up to a year.

★ **Note:** You can save up the zest from the lemons as it becomes available—just set it aside on a wire rack as you use up your lemons and proceed when you have enough to blend.

Fennel Stalks and Fronds

One of the first cooking classes I taught was all about fennel—my local farmers were growing it, but not many local eaters knew how to work with it. If you're not used to cooking with fennel, it can be hard to know how to break it down. Is it grown for its fronds, which look so much like dill? Or the tall, leggy stalks? Or the fat, juicy bulb at the root end? The answer is "yes" to all three.

Buying: Fennel sold in grocery stores often has had its fronds and stalks removed so that just the bulb remains. If you are shopping in the farmers' market, chances are the fennel you see there will be fully intact. The full fennel should have three healthy components—the fronds should be wispy and bright green, the stalks should be firm, and the bulb should feel heavy and be bright white to cream without a lot of yellow or brown, which indicates age. Older fennel is okay to eat but loses flavor over time.

Storing: Once home, wrap the entire fennel plant in damp paper towels or a reusable plastic bag and store in the crisper drawer for no more than several days.

Prepping: All parts of the fennel are great in a variety of dishes where they lend an exotic, licorice-like flavor—you just have to know where to use each bit. The fronds do act a lot like dill and you can use them as you would that delicate herb. Snip them off the bulb and use whole sprigs as a garnish or work

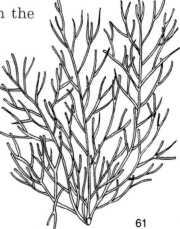

them into your herbal repertoire, anywhere that you would use dill or other tender herbs, such as the Fennel Frond Dip (page 65).

The stalks have a lot of flavor but can be tough and fibrous. They are best used in stocks and soups where you can enjoy their taste and avoid their chew, or in long cooking braises where the time and heat will temper their texture.

The bulb is the part of the plant called for most frequently in recipes and it's a real prize. You can serve the vegetable raw, where that anise taste will be most pronounced and the crunchy, peppy texture is a delight. Cooked, fennel bulbs have a fantastically mellow but still interesting subtle licorice flavor. While not a bad match for any roasted meat or even other roasted vegetables, fennel just sings its heart out when paired with fish.

Fish on a Fennel Bed

The fennel stalks add a lovely hint of flavor to the fish without overpowering it. If you've ever grilled or roasted fish on a cedar plank, it's the same theory—the stalks will "inform" the fish, as chefs say, transferring a subtle licorice flavor as a background note to the meal. This recipe calls for roasting the fish in the oven—an easy midweek meal solution—but you can also cook the fish on the grill. Just lay the fennel stalks on the grill and place the fish on top of them to cook.

You can stop there, using just the stalks, or sprinkle the fish with chopped fennel fronds after roasting to up the anise ante.

Note: For sustainable fish options in your area, see Monterey Bay Seafood Guide http://www.seafoodwatch.org.

Makes 4 servings

6 fennel stalks (5 to 6 inches long)

1¼ pounds (1- to 1½-inch-thick) fish fillets

2 tablespoons olive oil

Salt and freshly ground black pepper

1 lemon

1 tablespoon chopped fennel fronds, for garnish (optional)

➡ Preheat the oven to 400°F.

➡ Arrange the stalks in the center of a baking pan to make a sort of fennel raft. Rub the fillets all over with 1 tablespoon of the olive oil and a sprinkle of salt and pepper. Lay the fillets on the fennel, leaving ½ inch of space between them. Place the pan on the center rack of the oven. Roast until the fish is cooked through, 10 to 15 minutes (the fish will be nearly opaque at the center). Transfer the fish from the pan to a serving platter or individual plates, drizzle with the remaining tablespoon of olive oil and a squeeze of lemon, and garnish with the fennel fronds, if using.

Court Bouillon

One of the first "grown-up" dinner parties I attended was on a trip to Paris to visit a friend who was living there. The other guests and I had arrived and were sipping our cocktails while the host was keeping us wildly entertained with stories of his misadventures as an American in Paris. We were having a great time and were well into cocktail hour. Although the apartment smelled divine, it looked to me as if dinner prep hadn't even started.

It was a lesson in do-ahead entertaining when our host casually made his way over to the stove, brought a pot of liquid to a simmer, tossed in several bowls of cleaned fish, and fifteen minutes later announced that dinner was served. Steaming bowls of gorgeous poached fish in a rich broth, topped with a dollop of creamy, garlicky aioli, accompanied simply by a hunk of crusty French bread and a nice big salad, made for a delicious, satisfying and elegant meal that came together in a flash. All made possible by the court bouillon that he had cleverly made ahead.

This deeply flavored fish stock is very common in France. It's a terrific base to have on hand for your next "grown-up" dinner party, or anytime.

Makes 2 quarts bouillon

1 cup dry white wine, such as sauvignon blanc

2 fennel stalks

1 celery stalk

1 carrot

1 leek

1 garlic clove

1 bay leaf, fresh if possible, or 2 dried

3 sprigs fresh thyme, or ½ teaspoon dried

1 teaspoon salt

3 black peppercorns

➡ In a large saucepan, bring the wine and 7 cups of water to a boil. Add the remaining ingredients. Lower the heat and simmer for 30 minutes. Remove from the heat and allow to cool for an hour. Strain. Use immediately or cool, cover, and refrigerate for up to 3 days or freeze for 3 months.

➡ continues

COURT BOUILLON *continued*

★ **Note:** To poach fish in the court bouillon, bring the liquid to a low simmer (bubbles are gently rising and popping on the surface). Add any fish or shellfish of your choice and return the heat to just under a simmer (the water is swirling, but not bubbling). Do not boil, as the high temperature will toughen your fish. Cook until the fish is nearly opaque all the way to the center. If you are serving the fish without the broth, you can cool, cover, and refrigerate it for 2 to 3 days or freeze it and use the broth again; it will be even more flavorful.

Fennel Frond Dip

The bright, light flavor of the fennel and the earthy flavor of the beans and pine nuts, also called pignoli, make for a dip that plays well with many of your party dippers. Serve it with crostini, carrot sticks, steamed artichoke leaves, or tortilla chips. Or use it as a spread for a chicken or turkey sandwich.

Makes 1½ cups dip

1 (15-ounce) can cannellini beans, drained and rinsed

¼ cup fennel fronds

1 garlic clove

¼ cup olive oil

¼ cup freshly squeezed lemon juice (from 1 to 2 lemons), with their zest

Salt and freshly ground black pepper

➡ In a blender or food processor, puree the beans, fronds, garlic, olive oil, and lemon juice until smooth. Season with salt and pepper and serve.

➡ The dip keeps, covered and refrigerated, for 2 to 3 days.

Garlic Scapes

Garlic what? Garlic scapes are the green, snakelike flower stalks that sprout out of hard-neck garlic plants. They need to be trimmed away by the farmer so that all the energy (and taste) from the growing plant goes into the developing garlic bulb.

Previously unknown to all but growers and their groupies, garlic scapes have become more popular at farmers' markets. I've even seen them pop up in the occasional grocery store. It's no wonder they are developing such a strong following—they're versatile, keep well, and have fabulous flavor. Raw, they are pungent like garlic from the bulb—super in pesto. Cooked, they have the taste and texture of asparagus sautéed in a little garlic—heavenly. They also make a pretty neat pickle—a bonus.

Buying: Fresh scapes are green and succulent all the way from cut end to tip. Older ones will wither and become woody as they age.

Prepping: Some cooks use the whole scape, but I prefer to trim mine before using them in recipes, particularly if they were harvested a little later and have begun to mature. Just cut off the end, right below the seedpod, as that part and the section of scape above it can be bitter and stringy.

Storage: Scapes last a good long time. Just toss them in the crisper drawer, where they will keep for a week or more.

Then jump into the great e-scape with one of these recipes (sorry, couldn't help myself).

Pasta with Sautéed Garlic Scapes

It sounds hip, yet it's so easy. This pasta cooks up in a flash. The scapes are tender with only a hint of garlic flavor. You can add more punch, if you like, by supplementing the sauté with a few sliced garlic cloves. Or just leave it as is for a more mellow dish that the whole family will dig.

Makes 4 servings

8 ounces pasta, any shape

3 tablespoons olive oil

2 cups chopped garlic scapes (16 to 18 scapes)

2 to 4 garlic cloves, sliced (optional)

1 cup cherry tomatoes, such as Sungold

4 ounces Parmigiano-Reggiano cheese, grated (about 1 cup)

Pinch of red pepper flakes (optional)

Salt and freshly ground black pepper

➡ Boil the pasta according to the package directions. Drain and set aside, reserving 1 cup of pasta water.

➡ Sauté the scapes and garlic in the olive oil in a medium-size sauté pan over medium heat until the scapes are tender, 5 to 7 minutes. Add the tomatoes to the pan and sauté 1 to 2 minutes. Add ½ cup of water and simmer until the tomatoes burst, 2 to 3 minutes. Remove from the heat. Whisk in ½ cup of the cheese. Toss the scape mixture with the drained pasta, adding a splash more pasta water if needed to loosen it. Add a few red pepper flakes, if using, season with salt and pepper, and stir to combine. Divide among four bowls and pass the extra cheese for topping.

Pickled Scapes

When in doubt, pickle it! These cold-pack pickles, as vegetables that go into the pickling jar raw are called, are easy to put together. The coils of scapes are pretty in the jar and no chopping means that the prep is a snap. Serve these at your next picnic.

Makes 4 pints scapes

2 pounds garlic scapes

1 teaspoon mustard seeds

1 teaspoon celery seeds

8 peppercorns

4 garlic cloves, sliced

2 cups water

4 cups white distilled vinegar

2 tablespoons granulated sugar

2 tablespoons salt

- ➡ Tightly coil the garlic scapes and pack them into four clean, hot pint-size canning jars, leaving 1 inch of space between the top of the scapes and the top of the jar. Divide the mustard seeds, celery seeds, peppercorns, and garlic cloves equally among the four jars. Bring the water, vinegar, sugar, and salt to a boil and simmer to dissolve the sugar and salt, 1 to 2 minutes. Ladle the hot brine into the scape-filled jars to cover the scapes by ½ inch. Use a clean wooden skewer or chopstick to release any trapped air and top up with more brine, if necessary, to reach a ½-inch headspace between the top of the liquid and the top of the jar. Wipe the rims clean. Place lids on top and screw canning jar bands on just fingertip tight—that is, just until the rings meet resistance when twisted on, using only your fingertips.
- ➡ Use canning tongs to submerge the jars in boiling water to cover by 2 inches in a canner or pot fitted with a false bottom and cover with lid. Process by boiling for 15 minutes. Turn off the heat and allow the jars to rest for 5 minutes. Use canning tongs to transfer the jars from the boiling water to a towel-covered surface. Allow to cool for 24 hours. Test the seals by removing the ring and gently but firmly pushing up on the jar lid. If seal is secure, store the pickles in a cool, dark place for up to a year. If the seal has failed, store the pickles in the refrigerator for up to 3 weeks.

Scape Pesto

This is a great recipe to make when you only have a small amount of scapes on hand. Everyone loves pesto and the garlicky flavor of the scapes is right at home in this sauce. Use it on sandwiches, in pasta, or to flavor a pot of rice, or slather it on crostini and top with some chopped tomato for an easy app.

Makes 2 cups pesto

½ pound garlic scapes, roughly chopped, flower bulbs trimmed and discarded

1 cup olive oil

¼ cup pine nuts (also called pignoli)

1 cup fresh basil leaves

2 ounces Parmigiano-Reggiano cheese, grated (about ½ cup)

Salt and freshly ground black pepper

➡ In a blender, puree the scapes and oil. Add the nuts and puree until smooth. Add the basil leaves and puree again. Blend in the cheese. Season with salt and pepper. Serve immediately or cover and refrigerate for up to 3 days.

Green Tomatoes

Tomatoes are one of the big lures of the farmers' market. Gorgeous greens, all manner of summer squash, earthy mushrooms, succulent stone fruit, even the first juicy berries—nothing draws eaters to the market like the promise of a straight-from-the-vine tomato. Everyone scrambles to get the biggest beefsteak, the most obscure heirloom, grape tomatoes, cherry tomatoes—market-goers buy up whole flats of them. But not so, lowly green tomatoes. They are the first tomatoes to take the stage at the beginning of the season and the last to take a bow at the end of it. Yet green tomatoes have a hard time finding an audience. Sure, they are not as yielding as their fully ripened market superstars. But green tomatoes can be showstoppers in their own right.

The taste and texture of a green tomato is very different from the fruit when it is ripe. Green tomatoes are tart and tangy. They have a crunchy bite that one doesn't expect. Rather than seeing those qualities as liabilities, view them as bonuses. Because green tomatoes are nice and tart, they can stand up to other bold flavors and rich sauces, such as the Spicy Rémoulade that follows, which would overwhelm a fruit that is in full blush. Their firm texture allows for possibilities, such as frying and pickling, that would flat-out wilt and wither a peak-of-season tomato.

Buying: Buy 'em early in the season before they ripen or snatch them from the garden before Jack Frost gets his grip on them, but buy those green tomatoes and eat 'em up!

When selecting green tomatoes, it's important to choose those that are truly green, without even the faintest pink. Tomatoes that are even beginning to ripen will not give you the same results as a true greeny. Once your tomato begins to blush, best to leave it on the windowsill until it's red all over and enjoy as you would a vine-ripened fruit.

Storage: Once you bring your green tomatoes home, cook with them immediately. Tomatoes, even off the vine, will continue to ripen and soften. You'll be left with tomatoes that aren't sturdy enough for green tomato recipes but also lack the fully developed taste of one allowed to ripen in the field.

Prepping: Green tomatoes are prepped just like their fully ripe counterparts. Cut out the cores and proceed with your recipe.

Fried Green Tomatoes

The southern half of my soul demands regular feedings of this iconic Dixie treat. I can think of no better breakfast than fried green tomatoes, scrambled eggs, and grits. With bacon. And a biscuit. Maybe some nice sausage gravy, too. Or just fried green tomatoes with a nice Spicy Rémoulade Sauce in which to dip them. Or on a sandwich with bacon and lettuce. Oh, I love my BLFGT. Oh, I love my Fried Green Tamaytahs.

Makes 4 servings

SPICY RÉMOULADE

1 cup mayonnaise, preferably homemade (page 165)

2 tablespoons Creole or Dijon mustard

1 tablespoon freshly squeezed lemon juice

1 teaspoon Worcestershire sauce

1 tablespoon ketchup

1 teaspoon hot sauce, such as Crystal or Tabasco

2 scallions, finely minced

2 tablespoons minced fresh parsley

Salt and cayenne pepper

■ *continues*

FRIED GREEN TOMATOES continued

TOMATOES

2 medium-size to large green tomatoes

1 cup all-purpose flour

2 large eggs

1 cup fine cornmeal

1 cup corn flour

Salt and freshly ground black pepper

Neutral flavored oil, such as organic canola, enough to coat the bottom of a

    medium-size skillet by ¼ inch

➡ Make the rémoulade: In a small bowl, whisk all the ingredients to combine. Cover and refrigerate for at least an hour and up to 3 days.

➡ Make the tomatoes: Using a small, sharp paring knife, core the tomatoes. Cut the tomatoes into ½-inch slices equatorially and set aside. Arrange three shallow bowls in front of you, placing the flour in one, whisking the eggs in the second, and combining the cornmeal and corn flour in the third. Season the tomato slices with salt and pepper. One at a time, dip a tomato slice in the flour, knock off any excess, dip it in the egg wash, and then coat it in the corn mixture. Lay the coated tomato slice on a cookie sheet and proceed with the remaining tomato slices.

➡ Heat the oil in a medium-size skillet over medium heat until shimmering. Working in batches, use tongs to carefully lay four or five breaded tomato slices in the oil, being careful not to crowd the pan. Fry until golden, 3 to 4 minutes. Using tongs, carefully turn the slices over and fry on the other side for 2 to 3 minutes. Transfer to a wire rack to drain. Repeat with the remaining tomato slices. Season with salt and pepper and serve immediately with a dollop of rémoulade on the side.

Pickled Green Tomatoes

I don't usually like sweet pickles, but the heat from the chilis cuts the cuteness here, for a pickle that's sweet, sour, spicy, and just right. The sugar also helps preserve the color and texture of the tomatoes (as it does for any canned produce), so your pickles might dull to a mellow olive color but won't go an unappealing gray. They maintain a nice snap, too, as sugar toughens the cell walls of fruits and vegetables, so they don't turn to mush in the jar. You can reduce the sugar, but the tomatoes won't be as lovely or as pleasing to the tooth.

The other important ingredient here is the vinegar, which packs the acidic punch to allow for safe canning. Make sure that the vinegar you are using has a 5 percent acidity; the bottle's label will indicate that it does. Keep those things in mind and get pickling!

Makes 4 quarts tomatoes; can be doubled

4 pounds green tomatoes, cored, medium-size tomatoes cut in half, large tomatoes quartered

1 pound hot Italian peppers, halved lengthwise

8 garlic cloves, peeled

2 medium-size onions, peeled and quartered longitudinally

2 quarts cider vinegar (5% acidity)

2 cups light brown sugar

2 tablespoons salt

2 teaspoons ground allspice

1 tablespoon mustard seeds

½ teaspoon ground cloves

1 teaspoon whole black peppercorns

→ Divide the tomatoes, peppers, garlic, and onions equally among four hot, quart-size canning jars, being sure to pack the jars snuggly but not so tightly that liquid cannot circulate. Leave 1 inch of space between the top of the vegetables and the top of the jar.

→ Bring the vinegar, brown sugar, salt, and spices to a boil, simmering to dissolve the salt and sugar, 1 to 2 minutes. Ladle the hot brine over the packed vegetables, leaving a ½-inch headspace between the top of the liquid and the top of the jar.

→ continues

PICKLED GREEN TOMATOES *continued*

- Use a clean wooden skewer or chopstick to release any trapped air and top up with more brine, if necessary, to reach ½ inch of headspace between the top of the liquid and the top of the jar. Wipe the rims clean. Place lids on top and screw canning jar bands on just fingertip tight—that is, just until the rings meet resistance when twisted on, using only your fingertips.
- Use canning tongs to submerge the jars in boiling water to cover by 2 inches in a canner or pot fitted with a false bottom and cover with lid. Process by boiling for 20 minutes. Turn off the heat and allow the jars to rest for 5 minutes.
- Use canning tongs to transfer the jars from the boiling water to a towel-covered surface. Allow to cool for 24 hours. Test the seals by removing the ring and gently but firmly pushing up on the jar lid. If the seal is secure, store the pickles in a cool, dark place for up to a year. If the seal has failed, store the pickles in the refrigerator for up to 3 weeks.

Salsa Verde

Salsa verde is traditionally made with tomatillos, Mexican husk tomatoes, but green tomatoes make a fine substitute. I char the tomatoes, chilis, and onions to soften them all up and give the salsa a dose of sweetness. The charring also gives the salsa a nice, smoky flavor.

Makes four 8-ounce jars

½ pound chili peppers, such as jalapeño or poblano

4 pounds green tomatoes

1 pound yellow onions, quartered

1 tablespoon neutral oil, such as organic canola

2 garlic cloves, peeled

1 cup distilled white vinegar (5% acidity)

¼ cup chopped fresh cilantro

1 teaspoon salt

- Preheat the broiler. Lightly oil the peppers, tomatoes, and onion wedges with the oil. Arrange the peppers on a baking sheet and broil 3 to 4 inches from the element until blackened in spots, 3 to 5 minutes. Turn the peppers over and blacken on the other side. Transfer the peppers to a small

→ *continues*

bowl and cover to steam them for 5 minutes. Uncover the peppers and, when cool enough to handle, slip off the charred skins and remove the stems and seeds. Set aside.

➡ While the peppers are steaming and cooling, broil the tomatoes and onions in the same manner, making sure that all are well blistered.

➡ Puree the charred and peeled peppers, tomatoes, and onions with the garlic and vinegar in a blender or food processor, working in batches if necessary, and transfer to a large, nonreactive saucepan. Bring to a boil, lower the heat, and simmer until thickened, about 10 minutes. Stir in the cilantro and salt and remove from the heat. Allow to cool to room temperature and refrigerate, covered, for up to 5 days.

➡ Or can the salsa, using the boiling-water method: Ladle into clean, hot half-pint canning jars, leaving ½ inch of headspace. Release any trapped air by swirling a clean chopstick or wooden skewer along the inside of the jar. Wipe the rims clean. Place lids on top and screw canning jar bands on just fingertip tight—that is, just until the rings meet resistance when twisted on, using only your fingertips.

➡ Use canning tongs to submerge the jars in boiling water to cover by 2 inches in a canner or pot fitted with a false bottom and cover with lid. Process by boiling for 15 minutes. Turn off the heat and allow the jars to rest for 5 minutes. Use canning tongs to transfer the jars from the boiling water to a towel-covered surface. Allow to cool for 24 hours. Test the seals by removing the ring and gently but firmly pushing up on the jar lid. If the seal is secure, store the salsa in a cool, dark place for up to a year. If the seal has failed, store the salsa in the refrigerator for up to 3 weeks.

Herbs and Flowers

There's something very forest-witch about cooking with herbs. Particularly when you are harvesting your own from the garden. "A pinch of thyme, a leaf of bay will make dull meals go away!" All right, it's not much of an incantation, but then again, I am but a humble kitchen witch.

Herbs and flowers can turn dishes from frog to prince rather magically, indeed. A roasted chicken is an honorable thing, but stuff that bird full of stems and sprigs of whatever sturdy herb you have on hand—rosemary, thyme, marjoram, oregano—and that meal is ready for company. Even desserts can be transformed from fine to fantastic by adding some unexpected herbs. Try adding lavender or rosemary to a basic shortbread recipe—phenomenal! The transformative power of herbs allows you to riff on simple recipes, turning a short list of can-do meals into an expansive repertoire of dishes—no wand necessary.

Buying: When shopping for herbs, you want to look for lively-looking bunches. Leaves and needles should be fresh and sprightly. Give one a little pinch—it should release its fragrance. Pass by any bunches that are dull and certainly any bunches that have begun to brown or wilt. If you are gathering flowers or herbs from fields or gardens, be sure they haven't been sprayed with fertilizers or pesticides.

Storing: It's easy when you are buying herbs to waste a lot of them. Your recipe calls for such a small amount, the rest of the bunch gets tossed in the crisper drawer, and the next time you think about it is when you find yourself playing "guess what this mush used to be." Drying and freezing herbs are two easy ways to make sure that they don't wind up in the bin.

DRYING HERBS

Herbs are easy to dry. You can bind large bunches of them with a length of twine around the stems and hang them upside down until brittle. Or lay them out on racks where they will get good air circulation. When they are fully dry, crumble the leaves off the stems and store in an airtight container for up to 6 months. If you are drying multiple herb varieties, label the bunches so you can keep track of what's what. You can substitute dried herbs for fresh in many recipes, using a 1:3 ratio (1 teaspoon of dried for every 3 teaspoons [which equals 1 tablespoon] of fresh herbs called for).

FREEZING HERBS

Herbs don't take well to very cold temperatures. They go all slimy upon defrosting. Better to puree them with a glug of water or oil, divide them among the compartments of an ice cube tray and, when frozen solid, transfer to an airtight container and freeze for up to 3 months. Defrost before blending into sauces, dips, and marinades or tossing with hot pasta or rice, or add directly to simmering stews and soups.

Nasturtium Capers

Nasturtium is the gorgeous flowering vine that keeps on giving; it's lovely in the garden, sending off cascades of bright hot-colored flowers. The leaves are fine to eat and taste a great deal like peppery watercress. The flowers are not only pretty but also edible, bringing a spicy bite to salads or as tasty garnishes for any dish that could use a pop of flavor and color. Once the flowers have faded, they leave behind little seedpods on the flower stems that, when pickled, taste distinctly like pickled capers. The pickling process is easy and the brined capers keep for ages, so it's well worth the time spent. I use them just as I would jarred capers—in tartar sauce, sprinkled on top of a fried chicken cutlet or fish fillet, or in a pan sauce for steak. Their burst of tang and sizzle is a treat to have in the pantry.

When gathering seedpods, select the bright, fresh green ones. Yellow, drying pods will be bitter and tough. You can scale this recipe up or down to reflect the abundance of your nasturtium pod harvest.

Makes ½ cup capers

¼ cup salt

2 cups water

½ cup nasturtium seed pods, washed thoroughly

1 cup distilled white vinegar (5% acidity)

2 tablespoons granulated sugar

➡ Combine the salt and water in a small saucepan and bring to a boil. Simmer for 1 to 2 minutes, until the salt is dissolved. Allow to cool to room temperature. Combine the salt brine and the pods in a jar or bowl, cover, and set aside for 48 hours. Drain and rinse the capers. Pack them into a pint-size jar. In a small saucepan, bring the vinegar to a boil. Add the sugar and simmer for 1 to 2 minutes, until the sugar is dissolved. Ladle the hot vinegar mixture over the capers. Allow to cool to room temperature, then refrigerate, covered, for at least 3 days and up to 6 months.

EATING NASTURTIUM

Nasturtium is a prolific plant that thrives in almost any climate. Even I, Goddess of the Black Thumb, have been able to raise profusions of these tolerant, tasty plants. Here are a few tips for enjoying them:

- Know where your plants come from—you don't want to eat those that have been sprayed so make sure that any garden from which you harvest is not using toxic applications and never eat plants that have been harvested roadside.
- Be sure to thoroughly wash before using, and shake out the flowers, which provide the perfect nesting place for garden critters.
- Use the leaves in recipes that have a fair amount of fat to balance their punch—in a well-dressed salad, on a cucumber and cream cheese sandwich, or as part of the L in a BLT, for a bite with bite.
- The flowers have a lot of flavor. The small ones can be eaten whole, but large ones may be too much of a blast to take in one bite. Pull them into petals, mince, or chiffonade to keep them from overpowering.
- The flowers' peppery taste isn't just for savory applications. Try them with chocolate desserts for a riff similar to a chili/chocolate combo.

Cilantro Stem Green Sauce

Cilantro stems are tender, flavorful, and edible. Unlike parsley stems, you can chop them right along with their leaves and add them to your recipe. Or you can whir them into submission, as in this recipe. I serve it at cookouts along with the grilled vegetables, steak, chicken—whatever I'm throwing on the flame. A little drizzle of this crowd-pleasing sauce on any of those dishes tastes great. It's also addictive when swiped on grilled bread—top with a few chopped tomatoes or a slick of goat cheese and you have an instant app.

Makes just under 1 cup sauce

¼ cup red wine vinegar or freshly squeezed lemon juice

Salt and freshly ground black pepper

½ cup fresh cilantro stems (from 1 bunch of cilantro)

½ cup olive oil or neutral oil, such as organic canola or grapeseed

½ teaspoon ground cumin

➡ In a blender or the mixing cup of a small food processor or immersion blender, combine the vinegar and a pinch of salt and pepper. Swirl a few times to dissolve the salt. Add the stems, olive oil, and cumin and puree. Adjust the seasoning. Serve immediately or cover and refrigerate for up to 3 days.

Rosemary Skewers

Who doesn't like food on a stick? The next time you make a batch of kebabs, trade in the typical wooden skewer for a rosemary stem. Save them up from the recipes that call for rosemary needles—it's okay if they dry out; the flavorful oil will remain. The woody herb will bring a delicious hint of Mediterranean flavor to any food with which you spear it. Choose long, sturdy branches for hefty meats, such as steak, lamb, and chicken. Smaller, more flexible skewers are best for softer foods, such as chunks of fish and vegetables like tomatoes and eggplant.

Makes 4 servings

4- to 6-inch fresh rosemary stems, leaves removed and reserved for another use

1 pound meat, chicken, or fish, cut into 2-inch cubes, *and/or*

1 pound vegetables, such as cherry tomatoes, button mushrooms, and/or zucchini,

    eggplant, or summer squash, cut into 2-inch cubes

2 tablespoons oil with a high flash point, such as grapeseed oil

Salt

➡ Submerge the rosemary stems in water for at least 30 minutes. Thread the meat and/or vegetables onto the skewers. If you have trouble piercing all the way through, you can run the food through with a meat thermometer first. Lightly brush the threaded skewers with oil and season with salt. Grill over medium-high heat or 3 to 4 inches from the broiler element until well charred on both sides and cooked through. The times will vary, depending on the ingredients you choose.

Parsley Stems

Parsley stems can be tough and are often discarded in favor of the tender leaves. But they are full of the same great, grassy-green flavor that gives a lift to so many dishes. The key is to extract the flavor from the stems or pulverize them to a pleasing texture. Here are several tasty ways to get that special parsley punch.

Parsley Soup

This soup doesn't just please the palate, it pleases the pocketbook. Made out of the stems from a bunch or two of parsley, it's a real penny-pincher. But you'd never know it. It looks beautiful in the bowl and, finished with a lashing of cream, it tastes rich, indeed.

Makes 4 servings

2 tablespoons unsalted butter

1 onion, diced

1 cup fresh parsley stems, chopped

1 pound starchy potatoes, such as russet, peeled and chopped (about 2 large)

    (see page 84 for ways to use up potato peels)

1 quart chicken stock (preferably homemade, see page 142) or water

Salt and freshly ground black pepper

¼ cup heavy cream (optional)

■ continues

PARSLEY SOUP *continued*

- ➡ Sauté the onion in the butter in a medium-size saucepan over medium heat until softened, 3 to 5 minutes. Add the parsley stems and sauté until tender, 1 to 2 minutes. Add the potatoes, stock, and a pinch of salt and pepper and bring to a boil. Lower the heat and simmer until the potatoes are falling apart, about 25 minutes. Remove from the heat.
- ➡ Puree in a regular blender or with an immersion blender until smooth. Return the soup to the pan, add the cream, if using, and simmer for 2 to 3 minutes to thicken. Adjust the seasoning and serve.
- ➡ The soup keeps, cooled, covered, and refrigerated, for 2 to 3 days, or frozen, without the cream, for up to 3 months. Reheat and add the cream, if using, before serving.

Parsley Oil

Painting with your food. It's a trend you see at a lot of high-end restaurants these days. Swirls and swipes, drizzles and drips of colorful, flavorful this and that on the plate bring extra hits of *pow* to your eyes and your taste buds. It looks complicated, but it's not hard to do. A drizzle of thinned raspberry jam over a dessert plate, a squiggle of flavored mayo next to some steamed vegetables, or a few dots of this parsley oil either on the plate, floating on a soup, or decorating a piece of roasted fish and your meals are high-end, too.

Makes about ½ cup parsley oil

½ cup fresh parsley stems

½ cup organic canola oil

- ➡ Puree the stems and oil in a small food processor or with an immersion blender. Set aside for 10 minutes and puree again. Strain through a fine-mesh sieve. Transfer to a small squeeze bottle for easy application or use a spoon to drizzle oil as a garnish. Keeps, covered and refrigerated, for up to 5 days. Bring to room temperature before using.

Supergreen Smoothie

Greens are great in a smoothie. Spinach, kale, and wheatgrass are common add-ins at the juice bar. But did you know that you could throw in a handful of greens that you would normally throw out? Strawberry and radish tops, beet greens, or celery leaves can all be whizzed up, often undetected by even the most sensitive palates (attention, guardians of veggie-hating kiddlets). Parsley is one such add-in that brings a boost to the beverage. Juice masters swear by the curative and nutritive properties of the herb. I'm just happy to see it go into my belly rather than into the trash.

Makes 1 serving

½ cup fresh parsley stems

1 apple, stemmed and roughly chopped

1 banana, peeled

➡ Place all the ingredients in a blender and puree until smooth. Thin with water, if necessary, and enjoy.

Potato Peels

I love the earthy taste of potato skins and often leave them on when preparing recipes such as roasted potatoes or even mashed, particularly if I am working with young or waxy potatoes that have thin skins. When my recipe calls for peeled potatoes, I still find ways to enjoy their earthy flavor, if not in the same dish.

Buying: You can use the peels from any potato in these recipes—waxy potatoes, such as fingerlings; starchy ones, such as russets; or all-purpose (halfway between waxy and starchy), such as Yukon golds. Whatever variety you choose, potatoes for these recipes should be firm with little sign of shriveling or rot. Cut away the occasional small eye or blemish. But avoid potatoes that have a green tinge—they have developed solanine, a bitter compound that may cause stomach upset (see more about green potatoes on page 87).

Storing: To prevent your potatoes from developing green skins, be sure to store them out of direct sunlight. A cool, dark place, such as a low cupboard or corner of your basement, is best. Never refrigerate potatoes. The cold temperatures will convert the tubers' starch to sugar.

Prepping: Anytime you intend to eat the skin of a potato, you need to make sure that the vegetable is well scrubbed. You want to remove any dirt still clinging to it. Potatoes are notorious for being heavily sprayed in the field. It's another reason to scrub them well. I prefer to buy organic or locally grown potatoes that are minimally sprayed, to limit my exposure to agricultural chemicals.

When using potato peels in your recipes, be sure that you hand peel the potatoes, rather than peel them with a vegetable peeler. You want to make sure you get wide strips of peel, not thin chips. It also doesn't hurt to have just a bit of potato flesh on the peel as well—not so much that they might be considered French fries, but just a thin layer to give your prepared peel dishes a toothsome bite. Without it, the peels can be too papery.

EAT IT UP! FIVE WAYS WITH POTATO PEEL CHIPS

* Use the thin chips to garnish soups—particularly great on potato leek soup.
* Top a jumble of roasted peels with grated cheese and bacon bits for nacho-less nachos.
* Fancy it up—top chips with a dollop of sour cream and smoked wild salmon or domestic roe.
* Sprinkle with mild chili powder and serve with ranch dressing for dipping—kids love it!
* Don't limit yourself to white potatoes—try sweet potatoes, too. Great roasted with a little cinnamon.

Rustic Potato Chips

Nothing says home economy like making potato chips out of your potato peelings. But the results taste rich indeed. You can flavor these any way you want—with chili or curry powder, your favorite rub or seafood seasoning, or just keep it simple with a sprinkle of salt and a few grinds of black pepper.

Makes about 4 servings

3 to 4 cups potato peels from well-scrubbed potatoes

2 tablespoons neutral oil, such as organic canola, safflower, or grapeseed

1 teaspoon salt

1 to 2 teaspoons of any flavorful spice, such as chili or curry powder (optional)

➡ Preheat the oven to 400°F.

➡ Press the peels between a couple of sheets of paper towel to remove excess moisture. Place on a cookie sheet and drizzle with the oil. Sprinkle with the salt and spice, if using. Toss to coat. Bake until the peels are crisp, about 30 minutes. Serve immediately or store in an airtight container for up to 2 days.

Potato Peel Soup

This soup was a belly-filling staple during the Depression, when eaters used up every last lick of their designated rations. Just because we live in easier times doesn't mean we have to throw out this clever idea for enjoying good food. After all, no one ever got rich throwing money away. Or potato peels.

You can enjoy this soup as is or enrich it with the various add-ins listed.

Makes 4 servings

2 tablespoons unsalted butter

1 onion, diced

2 cups potato peels from well-scrubbed potatoes

1 quart chicken or vegetable stock (for homemade, see pages 142 and 107)

¼ cup heavy cream (optional)

SUGGESTED ADD-INS

When pureeing: add 1 cup cooked broccoli, asparagus, or carrot

After pureeing: stir in 1 cup Cheddar cheese, ½ cup cooked chicken,

   or a handful of cooked peas

When garnishing: top the finished soup with crumbled bacon,

   chopped fresh chives, or scallions

➡ Sauté the onion in the butter in a medium-size saucepan over medium heat until translucent, 5 to 7 minutes. Add the potato peels and stock and simmer until tender, 15 to 20 minutes. Puree in a standard blender or with an immersion blender with the suggested pureeing add-ins, if using. Return the soup to the pot, if necessary, and add the cream and any of the suggested simmering add-ins, if using. Simmer for 1 to 2 minutes. Divide among four bowls, top with garnishes, if using, and serve.

➡ The soup keeps, cooled, covered, and refrigerated, for 2 to 3 days.

Potato Peel "Croutons"

Sometimes a nice, big salad is just the ticket. Tucking into a salad as my main course satisfies my craving for a clean, crunchy pile of greens, but I need to add some substance to satisfy my hunger, too. A grating of cheese, some nuts and seeds, or crunchy croutons do the trick. These "croutons" are toasted bits of potato peel that have been roasted with some garlic to give them that familiar salad-topping flavor. A great use of the smaller shavings of peel that are too small to make a chip.

Makes 2 cups "croutons"

2 cups potato peels from well-scrubbed potatoes

6 garlic cloves, unpeeled

2 tablespoons olive oil

Pinch of dried thyme

Salt and freshly ground black pepper

1 ounce Parmigiano-Reggiano cheese, grated (about ¼ cup)

➡ Preheat the oven to 275°F.

➡ Toss the potato peels and garlic cloves with the oil, thyme, and salt and pepper to taste. Arrange in a single layer on a rimmed cookie sheet. Roast until crisp, about 20 minutes, tossing occasionally to ensure even cooking. Remove from the oven and immediately toss with the cheese. Use to top salads and casseroles. Can be stored in an airtight container for up to 1 week.

AVOIDING GREEN POTATO PEELS

Green eggs and ham, great. Green potatoes, not so much. Potatoes turn green when they are exposed to sunlight. This can happen in the field, if the spuds are too close to the surface or if the field has some cracks in it that have let in the light. It can also happen in the store or at home if the vegetable is exposed to too much light. The green is actually chlorophyll, which is in itself harmless. But it indicates another compound that develops when potatoes are exposed to light—solanine. Solanine is colorless but can be toxic, particularly if consumed in quantity. If your potatoes have a few areas of light green discoloration, you can trim that bitter part away and proceed with your recipe. But if the entire skin is green or the green color penetrates deep into the flesh, it is best to discard the whole potato, as those are indications that the vegetable has been exposed to enough light for a high level of solanine to be present. You can avoid this at home by always storing your potatoes in a cool, dark place or wrapping them in a brown paper bag.

Pumpkin Seeds

Jack-o'-lanterns are lovely. Cleaning out the pumpkin guts, though, can put you off your gourd. The reward for this not-so-super task, however, is the plump, delicious seeds, also called pepitas, which can be eaten straight up as a snack or included with great success in a variety of recipes.

Buying: There are two varieties of pumpkin seeds—those that have hulls (the white outer shell) and hull-less, also called "naked" seeds. If you are gleaning seeds from a carving or pie pumpkin, chances are the seeds have hulls. The hull-less variety comes from gourds known as "oil seed pumpkins" that are grown specifically for their seed, the fat of which is easily extracted. These oil seed pumpkins have a rather bland flesh and are not widely available.

Storing: Pumpkins can be kept for several months in a cool root cellar. At room temperature, they deteriorate much more quickly—within several weeks. Cut as a jack-o'-lantern, you can expect a pumpkin to last only several days in warm temperatures before slowly melting into squirrel bait. Hunks of edible pumpkin will keep for several days, wrapped well and refrigerated. Seeds can be covered and refrigerated for a day or two before proceeding with your recipe.

Prepping: If you've ever carved a pumpkin before, you know how to remove the seeds. Cut a hole in the top, reach in and scrape out the lovely gobs of pulp and seeds with your hand or a large spoon. Transfer all the pulp to a large cookie sheet and tease out the large clumps of seeds. Rinse the seeds in a colander to remove the finer strings of pulp and any sticky residue. At this point, you can simply roast the seeds, hull and all, and enjoy them as a snack (page 90). If you are going to use the seeds in recipes, it's best to remove the hull.

To remove the hull of pumpkin seeds, arrange a single layer of seeds on a sheet of parchment or waxed paper. Roll over the seeds with a heavy rolling pin or empty wine bottle to crack the shells. Be careful not to crush the meat of the seeds. Transfer the cracked pumpkin seeds to a large pot of boiling water and simmer for 30 minutes. Remove the pot from the heat and skim off the empty shells, which will be floating. Drain the now hull-less seeds. Transfer to a large cookie sheet and pat dry with paper towels. Allow to air dry and then proceed with your recipe or store in the refrigerator for up to a month.

Roasted Pumpkin Seeds

You can roast pumpkin seeds with or without their shells. Kids love to snack on them, shells intact—something about nibbling and spitting that's right up their alley. You can flavor the seeds simply with salt or with one of the spice combos I've listed, for a great homemade snacking treat.

Makes 1 cup seeds

1 cup pumpkin seeds, hulled or hull-less (see page 89)

2 teaspoons olive oil

Salt

OPTIONAL FLAVORING

¼ teaspoon ground cinnamon combined with 1 tablespoon granulated sugar;

1 teaspoon chili powder;

1 teaspoon curry powder; or ½ teaspoon ground ginger combined with ½ teaspoon ground cumin

➡ To roast the pumpkin seeds with their hulls, preheat the oven to 275°F. Rinse the seeds in a colander, then boil in a large pot of salted water for 10 minutes. Drain. Arrange in a single layer on a rimmed cookie sheet. Roast for 30 to 40 minutes, until dry, tossing occasionally to ensure even cooking. Drizzle with the oil, sprinkle with salt and flavoring, if using, and roast for an additional 10 minutes, or until just beginning to brown. Remove from the oven and allow to cool to room temperature (the seeds will crisp as they cool), then store in an airtight container for up to 2 weeks.

➡ To roast hull-less pumpkin seeds, preheat the oven to 325°F. Toss the seeds with the oil, salt, and flavorings, if using. Arrange on a rimmed cookie sheet in a single layer. Roast for 10 minutes. Serve hot or allow to cool to room temperature and store in an airtight container for up to 2 weeks.

Candied Pumpkin Seeds

These candied seeds are delicious on their own—it's hard to keep your hand out of the bowl. But my favorite way to serve them is on a cheese platter, where their salty sweet flavor is the perfect counterpoint to rich cheeses. Try them with nutty firm cheeses, such as aged Gouda, or for a combo that is really off the charts, a nice funky blue cheese.

Makes 2 cups seeds

½ teaspoon ground cinnamon

½ teaspoon salt

½ teaspoon ground cumin

2 tablespoons unsalted butter

½ cup granulated sugar

1 cup shelled raw pumpkin seeds (also called pepitas)

➡ Combine the cinnamon, salt, and cumin in a small bowl and set aside. In a medium-size skillet, melt the butter over medium heat. Add the sugar and stir to combine. Lower the heat to medium-low and continue to cook, stirring constantly to avoid scorching, until the sugar melts and caramelizes, about 5 minutes. Remove from the heat. Add the spice mixture and stir to combine, moving quickly to avoid burning the spices. Add the pumpkin seeds and stir to coat. Transfer to a parchment-lined cookie sheet and use a spatula to spread the mixture into a thin, even layer. Allow to cool completely. Crumble the cooled mixture into bite-size pieces and serve, or store in an airtight container for up to 1 week.

Pumpkin Seed "Mole"

Moles, pronounced mo-lay, are traditional Mexican sauces made from a range of ingredients that can include chilis, nuts, vegetables, fruits, and spices. They span the culinary rainbow in color and flavor from the bright green tomatillo-based mole verde to the chocolate-enriched, almost black mole negro.

I call this sauce a "mole" in quotation marks because it's really a mash-up, putting to use my favorite ingredients from the different sauces rather than just staying true to one combination. That being said, every mole reflects the hand of the cook and a great deal of pride is taken in making the sauce one's own. Use this recipe as a starting point, but don't be afraid to tweak it to your taste. The best mole is your mole.

Makes about 1 quart mole

1 ancho chili, stemmed and seeded

1 tablespoon mild paprika

2 teaspoons ground cumin

2 teaspoons ground coriander

1 teaspoon dried oregano

1 tablespoon unsweetened cocoa powder

¼ cup shelled raw pumpkin seeds (also called pepitas)

2 tablespoons neutral oil, such as organic canola

1 onion, diced

1 mildly spicy chili, such as poblano, diced (about ¾ cup)

Salt and freshly ground black pepper

2 garlic cloves, minced

28 to 32 ounces whole canned tomatoes (preferably home-canned)

➡ Bring 2 cups of water to a boil. Remove from the heat and submerge the ancho in the hot water to soften. Set aside while you prepare the rest of the mole.

➡ Combine the spices, oregano, and cocoa powder in a small bowl and set aside.

➡ Toast the pumpkin seeds in a large, dry sauté pan over medium heat, tossing constantly to avoid burning the seeds, until lightly browned and fragrant, 3 to 5 minutes. Remove from the pan and set aside.

➡ *continues*

PUMPKIN SEED "MOLE" *continued*

➡ In the same pan over medium heat, sauté the onion and chili pepper, seasoned with salt and pepper, in the oil until softened, 5 to 7 minutes. Add the garlic and sauté until fragrant, about 1 minute. Add the spice mixture and sauté for about a minute to release their essential oils. Add the tomatoes, toasted seeds, and rehydrated ancho to the pan (reserve the soaking liquid) and stir to combine. Lower the heat and simmer until thickened, about 45 minutes, adding the reserved ancho soaking liquid or water to the pan as necessary to keep it from sticking. (Using the soaking liquid will up the heat ante, so use water for a milder mole). Remove from the heat and allow to cool slightly.

➡ Puree in a blender, working in batches if necessary. Thin with more of the soaking liquid or water as necessary to reach the consistency of a thick tomato sauce. Use immediately, store in the refrigerator for up to 5 days, or freeze for up to 6 months.

EAT IT UP! MOLE STASH

It's great to have a stash of mole in your freezer. Use it as a simmer sauce for chicken, pork, or vegetables; as a base for chili; or slathered on some tortillas for huevos rancheros.

Radish Tops

The first time I ate a radish top was at Blue Hill at
Stone Barns. I was with my friend, Nena Johnson,
who worked at Stone Barns at the time. We were
bellied up at the bar and the kitchen sent us out some
snacks. Gorgeous radishes straight from the field, greens
still attached. Nena took a root bite and then, pop, in went
the rest, greens and all. So, I downed my radish greens as
well. Spicy veg, spicy thought. It made me reconsider what we throw out.

Now when I see those plastic bags of topless globe radishes, ubiquitous
in the supermarket, I regard them with fair amount of contempt. Not only
are they missing a neat little flavor component, they are also lacking a key
indicator of freshness. Root vegetables, such as radishes and carrots, can stay
fresh looking long after they have been harvested. The greens, however, wilt
much more rapidly. Those leaves don't lie. Fresh greens equal fresh food.
And that's always something good to eat.

Buying: When shopping for radishes, choose those that have healthy, entic-
ing green tops. The greens should be perky with no sign of wilting or withering. And certainly with nothing black or decrepit looking about them.

Storing: Radishes will keep longer with their greens trimmed, so it's best to
remove them within a day or so of getting them home. Store the radish roots
in a reusable plastic bag or damp paper towels for up to a week. Greens cut
from their roots should be used within a day.

Prepping: Radish greens should be trimmed within ½ inch of the root. You
can then use them as your recipe dictates.

Tabbouleh with Radish Leaves and Feta

This Mediterranean grain salad is a great recipe to have under your belt. It keeps really well so you can make it ahead for easy entertaining or keep a batch in the fridge for a quick brown bag lunch option. Serve it as a side with any grilled or roasted meat or vegetables or add some cooked chicken, shrimp, or beans to make it into a satisfying meal. I like to add feta cheese to mine to give it a briny punch, but you can leave out the cheese for a vegan salad. Bulgur wheat is traditional, but if you don't have that on hand, you can substitute 3 cups of cooked quinoa.

Makes about 4 servings

1 cup bulgur wheat

1 small red onion or shallot, minced

¼ cup freshly squeezed lemon juice

Salt and freshly ground black pepper

¼ cup good-quality olive oil

¼ cup fresh mint, chopped

¼ cup radish leaves, minced

1 tomato, diced

1 cucumber, seeded and diced

½ cup feta cheese, crumbled

- To prepare the bulgur, place it in a medium-size heatproof bowl. Pour enough boiling water over the bulgur to cover by ½ inch. Cover the bowl and set aside until the bulgur is tender and plump, 15 to 20 minutes. Pour off any excess water.

- Combine the onion, lemon juice, and a pinch of salt and pepper in a medium-size bowl. Set aside while the bulgur soaks. (This brief soak in the acidic lemon juice will "pickle" the onions slightly, tenderizing them and mellowing their flavor.)

- Add the soaked bulgur to the lemon mixture and toss to combine. Add the oil and toss again. Add the remaining ingredients, except for the feta, and toss one final time. Top with the feta. Serve immediately or cover and refrigerate for up to 3 days.

Green Rice

This is a recipe that I have made with all kinds of tender herbs—parsley is great; cilantro tastes terrific, particularly when served alongside black beans. The radish tops bring a little heat to the game. If it's too much for your taste, you can use the radish tops in combination with either parsley or cilantro to tame them. Whatever herbs you use, the rice turns an attractive shade of green and the oil in the recipe keeps the grains from clumping up—two features that make this a perfect candidate for a buffet dish.

Makes 4 to 6 servings

1 cup uncooked long-grain rice

Salt

¼ cup olive oil

¼ cup radish tops or a combination of radish tops and fresh parsley or cilantro

Freshly ground black pepper

➡ Cook the rice like pasta: Bring a quart of water to the boil. Add a handful of salt to the water—it should taste as salty as the sea. Add the rice and simmer, uncovered, until the rice is tender, about 20 minutes. Drain the rice and return it to the pan. Cover and set aside for 5 minutes.

➡ Meanwhile, puree the greens and oil in a small food processor or blender. Toss the hot rice with the puree, adjust the seasoning, and serve.

Daikon Greens with Slippery Noodles

I love these noodles—they're one of those dishes that taste really exotic and cool but are super easy to make. I use rice noodles, the same kind you would use for pad thai, but if you can't find those, you can substitute fettuccine pasta. Whichever type of noodle you're using, it's important to rinse the cooked pasta to remove any excess starch—doing so keeps the salad from getting gluey and cools the noodles so they don't absorb all the sauce.

I am using the greens from daikon; they are more plentiful than the greens from red radishes and have a more delicate texture. You can substitute or supplement with other greens—such as beet or turnip greens—just be sure to chiffonade the leaves (see page 27) so that they become a part of the salad, not the focus.

Makes 4 to 6 servings

2 tablespoons rice vinegar or white wine vinegar

2 tablespoons soy sauce

Pinch of granulated sugar

¼ cup neutral oil, such as organic canola

1 tablespoon toasted sesame seed oil

Pinch of red pepper flakes (optional)

8 ounces dried rice noodles or fettuccine pasta

1 daikon radish, shredded on a box grater

2 carrots, peeled and shredded on a box grater

½ cup daikon or other greens, cut into chiffonade

2 scallions, finely sliced

➡ In a medium-size bowl, whisk together the vinegar, soy sauce, and sugar until the sugar is dissolved. Slowly whisk in the neutral and sesame oils. Add the pepper flakes, if using. Set aside.

➡ Bring a large pot of water to a boil. Add the noodles and boil for 5 minutes, until tender but still al dente, if using rice noodles, or according to package directions, if using fettuccine. Drain the noodles in a colander. Rinse the noodles in the colander with plenty of cool water. Drain thoroughly.

➡ Add the noodles to the dressing and toss to combine. Add the radish, carrots, greens, and scallions and toss again. Serve immediately.

Tomato Water

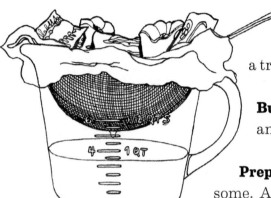

Tomato water is not the most common kitchen by-product but it's a treasure, indeed.

Buying: You can make tomato water from any ripe tomato—the riper the better.

Prepping: Here's how to get your hands on some. Anytime you are prepping fresh tomatoes, gather up the trimmings—the cores, the ends that you cut off, or any pulp that you might squeeze out of the fruit. Transfer them to a clean, airtight container and pop it in the freezer. When you have a nice accumulation of trimmings—at least a quart or so—you can make your water. Set a fine-mesh colander over a large bowl, transfer the frozen trimmings to the colander, and allow to defrost. The colander will catch the solids and, at the end of defrosting, you will have a bowl of tomato water.

Alternatively, you can use heat to extract your tomato water. This is the best method to use when you will have a large volume of trimmings all at once—when you are prepping tomatoes for canning, for example. Gather up all your trimmings—peels, cores, and so on—and transfer to a large pot. Add a cup of water for every gallon of trimmings. Cover and slowly bring to a simmer, being careful not to scorch the trimmings. Simmer until the trimmings are soft and have released their juice—about 20 minutes. Transfer to a colander set over a bowl. Press on the solids to remove as much juice as possible and proceed with your recipe.

You can also chop up all your trimmings or grind them in a food processor or blender—perhaps with some other good flavors such as a chili pepper, a bit of lemongrass, or a sprig of rosemary or thyme—and strain them through a colander lined with cheesecloth. Or you can simply run all your accumulated trimmings through a juicer.

Storing: Tomato water keeps in the refrigerator for up to 3 days or frozen for up to 3 months.

Tomato-tinis

Stronger than a Bloody, not as potent as a straight martini, this cocktail is just the thing to set the mood before a summer feast. Tomato may sound like an odd flavoring for a martini, but its sweetness really comes through here—tomato is a fruit, after all. The basil garnish reminds you of exactly where you are in the calendar—smack dab in the middle of summer. And if you have one of these in your hand, in the middle of a pretty good time, too.

Makes 2 cocktails

3 ounces vodka

1 ounce dry vermouth

4 ounces tomato water

Dash of herbal bitters

3 fresh basil leaves

➡ Chill two large martini or margarita glasses. Fill a cocktail shaker or small pitcher with ice. Add the vodka, vermouth, tomato water, and bitters and swirl for 60 seconds to chill thoroughly. Swipe the rims of the glasses with one of the basil leaves. Strain the cocktail into the glasses, dividing it evenly between the two. Garnish with the remaining basil leaves and enjoy.

Tomato Basil Granita

This granita is a great palate cleanser between courses or you can simply enjoy it as a cooldown on a hot summer's day. There is a fair amount of sugar, but it's a necessary ingredient that keeps the texture slushy. It's best to serve the granita within a day or two of putting it together. If it stays too long in the freezer, the shards of ice will find their way back together again and you will have a tomato basil berg.

Makes 4 servings

2 cups tomato water

1 cup granulated sugar

¼ cup plus 4 small fresh basil leaves

¼ cup freshly squeezed lemon juice

Pinch of salt

➡ Bring 1 cup of the tomato water to a boil. Add the sugar and ¼ cup of basil leaves and simmer until the sugar is melted, 1 to 2 minutes. Strain the syrup into a small, freezer-proof container, such as a small Pyrex or Tupperware container. Add the remaining cup of tomato water, the lemon juice, and the salt, stirring to combine. Put in the freezer for 1 hour. Use a fork to scrape any frozen crystals from the sides and bottom of the container and return it to the freezer. Repeat the process two times, freezing the liquid for an hour and scraping with a fork to break up the ice crystals. Divide among four serving dishes, garnish with leaves, and serve.

➡ The granita keeps, frozen, for 1 to 2 days before losing texture.

TOMATO LEAVES

Tomato leaf is one of my favorite smells—it's summer, garden, and al fresco dinners all in a single whiff. It's a nice fragrance, but is it good to eat? The jury is out on whether tomato leaves are toxic. Old wives' tales detail children falling ill from them and livestock dying from munching on tomato vines they come across. However, there is little science to support these stories. Some chefs add a few leaves to their tomato sauce to brighten its flavor and give it a fresh-picked taste. Call me superstitious, but I'm going to side with the grannies, and leave the tomato leaves to the compost.

Tomato Water "Ceviche"

This is a seafood cocktail designed for the ceviche-wary cook. Unlike the traditional ceviche, which uses chemistry to "cook" the raw fish in a strong citrus dressing, this recipe gently heats the ingredients in the tomato water so they are cooked in the traditional sense. The recipe uses the classic ceviche flavors—with hits of lime, chili, and cilantro—that make it such a popular Latin American dish. Domestic Gulf shrimp are my favorite in this dish.

Serves 4

2 cups tomato water

½ teaspoon salt

1 pound raw shrimp, shells on

2 tablespoons freshly squeezed lime juice (from 1 lime, zest reserved for another use
   [see page 57])

1 chili pepper, stemmed, seeded, and ribs removed and minced (jalapeño for mild to medium,
   serrano for medium to incendiary)

¼ cup minced fresh cilantro leaves and stems

2 tablespoons good-quality olive oil

Toasted baguette slices

➡ Have ready a medium-size bowl of ice water.

➡ Bring the tomato water and salt to a boil in a medium-size saucepan. Add the shrimp, lower the heat to a low simmer, and poach until the shrimp curl and the shells turn pink, 3 to 4 minutes. Using a slotted spoon, remove the shrimp from the poaching liquid, reserving it, and submerge the shrimp in the ice water. When the shrimp are chilled through, after about 5 minutes, drain, peel, and devein. Cover and refrigerate.

➡ Meanwhile, return the poaching liquid to a simmer until reduced by half, 8 to 10 minutes. Chill the reduced liquid by sitting your saucepan in the bowl of ice water or refrigerating for an hour.

➡ To serve, divide the shrimp among four plates. Combine the cooled poaching liquid and lime juice and pour it over the plated shrimp. Garnish with minced chili and cilantro. Drizzle with olive oil. Serve with toasted baguette slices for sopping up the spiked tomato liquid.

Watermelon Rinds

Watermelon rinds are a treasure hidden right in plain sight. Maybe because kids are taught to just eat the pink part of the fruit, we grow up thinking of the rind as something inedible. But they are terrific! Vastly different from the colored flesh of the fruit, they are almost vegetal in flavor—snappy and verdant, similar to cucumber. They hold up well when cooked, becoming translucent and jewel-like when they hit the heat.

Buying: Choose watermelons that have a significant rind. Not all watermelons do. If possible, check to see whether a sample melon has been cut to give you a peek inside or ask your farmer for a variety that has a nice, thick rind.

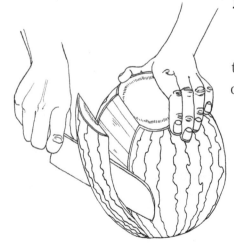

Prepping: Harvesting the rind takes a little effort, but it's so abundant you will have a big pile ready to go in no time. Here's how to get in there. First, wash your melon thoroughly with dish soap and water (this is a good practice anytime you slice a melon—or any fruit for that matter—as the skins can harbor a lot of bacteria that will be transferred to the cut fruit as you slice). Dry it off and place it on a cutting board. Using a large chef's knife, cut off both ends of the melon, deep enough to reveal the colored flesh. Set those aside. Turn the melon so that one of the flat sides is on the board. Cut down the melon from top to bottom, just where the rind meets the flesh, following the contour of the fruit as you go. Rotate the melon clockwise with each few cuts, to maintain a good angle for your knife work. When you are finished, you will have a sphere of melon flesh, multiple planks of rind and two bowl-like end pieces. Scoop any flesh out of the bowl ends and set it aside. Cut the bowl ends and planks into 1-inch-wide slices. Cut off the dark green skin with a knife or remove it with a vegetable peeler. Proceed with your recipe.

Storing: Treat prepped watermelon rind like chopped cucumber. It keeps, covered and refrigerated, for a day or two.

Pickled Watermelon Rind

These rinds taste more like candy than pickles. The watermelon rind goes a gorgeous translucent amber color. All sparkle and sweet and full of warm spices. These pickles are great any time of year, but look particularly festive on a holiday table—as equally at home on a cheese board as a dessert platter. They're just terrific.

Makes 4 pints rind

1 cup salt

4 pounds watermelon rind, pink flesh and green skin removed, cut into 1 by 2-inch slices

8 cups ice

■ continues

PICKLED WATERMELON RIND *continued*

8 cups granulated sugar

4 cups cider vinegar (5% acidity)

4 cinnamon sticks

1 teaspoon whole cloves

Zest of 1 lemon, cut into strips

- Combine 3 quarts of water with the salt in a large bowl, sink, or an impeccably clean cooler and stir to dissolve completely. Add the watermelon rind and ice and let sit for at least 8 hours and up to 12. Drain, rinse thoroughly, and drain again.

- Put the rind in a large pot with enough water to cover. Bring to a boil, lower the heat, and simmer for 10 minutes. It will soften a bit but still be quite firm. Drain and set aside.

- Combine the sugar, vinegar, 1 quart of water, and the cinnamon sticks, cloves, and lemon zest in a large, nonreactive pot and bring to a boil. Add the melon rind, return the heat to a boil, then lower the heat and simmer, partially covered, for 1 to 1½ hours, until the rind is tender and translucent.

- Ladle into bowls or jars, dividing the spices equally among them. Allow to cool, then cover and refrigerate for up to 3 weeks.

- Or can using the boiling-water method: Ladle the rinds* into clean, hot pint-size canning jars, covering the solids with ½ inch of liquid and leaving ½ inch of headspace between the top of the liquid and the top of the lid. Release any trapped air by swirling a clean chopstick or wooden skewer along the inside of the jar. Wipe the rims clean. Place lids on top and screw canning jar bands on just fingertip tight—that is, just until the rings meet resistance when twisted on, using only your fingertips.

- Use canning tongs to submerge the jars in boiling water to cover by 2 inches in a canner or pot fitted with a false bottom and cover with lid. Process by boiling for 10 minutes. Turn off the heat and allow the jars to rest for 5 minutes. Use canning tongs to transfer the jars from the boiling water to a towel-covered surface. Allow to cool for 24 hours. Test the seal by removing the ring and gently but firmly pushing up on the jar lid. If the seal is secure, store the pickles in a cool, dark place for up to a year. If the seal has failed, store the pickles in the refrigerator for up to 3 weeks.

---

* The flavor of the spices will intensify during storage. If you like a strong, spicy flavor to your pickle, remove the spices from the pickling liquid and divide them equally between your jars along with the rind. If you want a more subtle flavor you might want to leave them out of the canning jars. The spices can be rinsed, frozen, and, reused to infuse hot beverages such as tea, cider, or wine.

Curried Watermelon

This curry has a great balance of sweet and heat. The watermelon provides a light and lovely background and the chili kicks in just enough burn to bring the dish to life. Using the entire melon gives the curry a great combination of flavors and textures. Serve this summertime recipe with chicken or vegetables straight off the grill.

The recipe calls for ghee, the Indian version of clarified butter. It's available at many Asian markets.

Makes 6 servings

1 (3-pound) piece seedless watermelon

2 tablespoons ghee or organic canola oil

1 jalapeño chili, seeded and cut into ¼-inch slices

1 teaspoon cumin seeds

1 teaspoon coriander seeds

½ teaspoon ground turmeric

Salt and freshly ground black pepper

1 lime

➡ Prep the watermelon rind as described on page 102. Cut the rind and flesh into 1-inch pieces.

➡ In a medium-size saucepan, sauté the rind in the ghee until beginning to brown, 5 to 7 minutes. Add the jalapeño and sauté until fragrant, about 1 minute. Add the spices and stir to combine. Add 1 cup of water and cover the pot tightly. Simmer until the rind is tender, about 10 minutes. Add the watermelon flesh and continue to simmer until heated through. Season with salt and pepper, squeeze the juice from the lime over the top, and serve.

Thai Rind Salad

I love the combination of flavors in this dish. It's very similar to green papaya salad with its mix of sour, salty, and sweet. You could top it with some steamed fish or chicken to make it into a light but lovely meal for a hot summer's night.

Makes 4 side dish servings

2 cups watermelon rind, cut into matchsticks

　　(see page 102 for how to prepare watermelon rind)

¼ cup rice vinegar

2 tablespoons freshly squeezed lime juice

1 teaspoon nam pla*

1 teaspoon soy sauce

Pinch of salt

Pinch of granulated sugar

¼ cup neutral oil, such as organic canola

1 large cucumber, peeled, seeded, and cut into matchsticks

1 shallot, sliced thinly, rinsed, and drained

Pinch of red pepper flakes

¼ cup chopped peanuts

¼ cup chopped fresh cilantro

➡ Blanch the watermelon matchsticks. Drop them into a small pot of boiling water and simmer for 60 seconds. Use a slotted spoon to transfer them to a colander. Rinse under cold water. Drain, blot dry, and set aside.

➡ In a medium-size bowl, whisk the lime juice, nam pla, soy sauce, salt, and sugar until the salt and sugar are dissolved. Gradually whisk in the oil. Add the blanched watermelon rind, cucumber, shallot, and red pepper flakes. Toss to combine. Garnish with the peanuts and cilantro. Serve immediately.

---

* Nam pla, Thai fish sauce, is available in the Asian section of most grocery stores or from specialty Asian groceries.

Vegetable Stocks

Stocks are the best way to glean that last little bit of flavor from otherwise non-plate-worthy foods. Stems, peels, cobs, and skins—they all go into the pot and leave their flavor behind.

These vegetable stocks bring depth to any recipe that calls for liquid. They're essential in soups, stews, and risottos; make a fabulous deglazing liquid for a quick pan gravy; and bring a subtle layer of flavor when used to make rice, quinoa, and other grains. They're even nice sipped on their own when you are feeling under the weather, perhaps with a nice grating of ginger and a dash of hot sauce.

Stocks store beautifully. You can transfer them to airtight containers and freeze for up to six months. Or you can pressure can them and they will be shelf stable for up to one year.

Basic Vegetable Stock

To make a nice pot of stock, it helps to have a good amount of vegetable matter to get the flavor going. You don't have to start with fresh trimmings—you can gather them as you have them and then make a batch of stock once you have a pot full. Jacques Pépin offers the best way to do this: keep a clean, half-gallon carton in the freezer and add your trimmings to it as you prep your meals. An onion skin here, some carrot peelings the next night, leek greens, and on and on until the container is full. When you are ready to make your stock you can just peel away the paper carton, put your veggie berg in the pot, cover it with water, and crank up the heat.

➡ continues

BASIC VEGETABLE STOCK *continued*

There's a lot you can throw in the stockpot. But not all vegetables scraps are suitable. Cruciferous vegetables, such as broccoli, cabbage, cauliflower, and Brussels sprouts, will dominate the broth, infusing it with a distinctly cabbagy taste and smell. Peppers, as well, can have too pronounced a flavor for stock. But that still leaves so many options, including ends, peels, and trimmings from potatoes, carrots, celery, garlic, leeks, shallots, parsley, scallions, mushrooms, and tomatoes. Just make sure that you have a good balance of ingredients, for the most complex flavor.

Makes about 1 quart stock

4 cups assorted vegetables scraps

1 bay leaf

Salt and freshly ground black pepper

➡ Place the scraps in a medium-size saucepan and cover with cold water by 2 inches. Add the bay leaf and salt and pepper to taste. Slowly bring to a simmer over medium heat. Lower the heat and gently simmer for 1 hour. (Avoid the temptation to simmer for an extended period of time. Vegetables that simmer for more than 2 hours will taste bitter indeed.)

➡ Remove from the heat and strain through a colander into a heatproof bowl. Compost the spent vegetables. Set the stock aside to cool to room temperature and allow any grit to settle. Carefully pour off the broth, leaving any sediment behind.

➡ Store in the refrigerator for up to 5 days or freeze for 6 months. Pressure can and your stock will be shelf stable for up to 1 year.

Mushroom Stock

Trimming mushrooms often means that only the caps get used in your recipe. Seems a horrible waste to just pitch such a volume of that earthy mushroom flavor. Simmer up your stems and you can capture that mushroom taste and leave the fibrous plant material behind. You don't have to use anything other than mushroom stems in this stock, but I find that the addition of some other vegetable material and a few aromatics gives the broth a nice boost.

Making the stock is so easy that I often whip up a batch on the back burner while I prepare the rest of my mushroom dish, killing two birds with one stone. If multitasking isn't for you, or you don't have the critical mass of trimmings needed for a pot of stock, just put them in an airtight container in the freezer and then proceed when you have enough to make it worth the effort.

Makes about 1 quart stock

3 to 4 cups mushroom stems, from any variety of mushrooms

1 cup vegetable scraps, such as onion skins, celery ends, or carrot peels (optional)

1 bay leaf (optional)

Salt and freshly ground black pepper

➡ Place all the ingredients, except for the salt and pepper, in a medium-size saucepan. Add enough water to cover by 2 inches. Bring to a simmer over medium heat. Lower the heat and gently simmer for 1 hour. Remove from the heat. Strain through a fine-mesh sieve into a heatproof bowl. Season with salt and pepper to taste. Set aside to cool to room temperature and allow any grit to settle. Carefully pour off the broth, leaving any sediment behind.

➡ Store in the refrigerator for up to 5 days or freeze for 6 months. Pressure can and your stock will be shelf stable for up to 1 year.

Corn Stock

Corncobs don't look like much, but you'll be surprised at how much corn flavor is in the cob. Corncob stock is sweet and milky, so it not only brings a little sugar to a dish, but a subtly silky texture as well. It's great used in risottos, soups, and stews, where the stock adds body and viscosity. Use it instead of water in polenta or grits to up the corn quotient of those porridges.

Corncobs are bulky to freeze and readily pick up the flavors of the fridge, so I don't recommend saving them up to make this stock. They are best simmered right after the kernels have been removed, or at most, with no more than a day's layover in the fridge.

Makes about 1 quart stock

At least 4 corn cobs, broken in half

Salt

- ➡ Place the cobs in a large saucepan or stockpot. Cover with cold water by 2 inches. Add a pinch of salt. Slowly bring to a simmer over medium heat. Lower the heat and gently simmer for 1 hour.
- ➡ Remove from the heat and strain through a colander into a heatproof bowl.
- ➡ Store in the refrigerator for up to 5 days or freeze for 6 months. Pressure can and your stock will be shelf stable for up to 1 year.

3 THE WHOLE BEAST

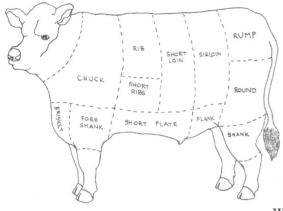

As chefs and eaters return to the traditional idea of fully utilizing all the food they harvest, "whole animal" dishes and menus have become increasingly common. The concept behind the effort is an earnest and important one—if we are going to raise animals for food, we should not only do it in a humane way but fully enjoy every bit of food made available by the process.

There are a lot of good books on the topic that will show you how to delve deeply into these farm-to-table techniques. They will teach you how to cure beef tongue, fry brains, tenderize trotters, and more. They are valuable resources worthy of many pages. Although I fully recommend them (see Resources, page 224, for a list), this section is not intended to be a deep DIY butchering lesson or guide to cooking the more exotic cuts.

The "Whole Beast" section that follows offers a start at eating up the things that frequently come our way—the fat from your roast, the bag of giblets in every market bird, the bones left behind from the family meal. It is by no means exhaustive and will not take you out of your way to go searching for good-quality offal. But I do hope that it helps you make use of the good things to eat that are already in your kitchen.

I always shop for sustainably raised meat from animals that have been treated well, have been fed well, and were humanely slaughtered. Such husbandry isn't just compassionate or good politics; it makes for more flavorful and more healthful meals. After all, you are not only what you eat, but what you eat, eats. A species-appropriate diet, including grass for ruminant animals, such as cows, sheep, and goats, and access to grass and insects for poultry is best. It gives them the highest quality of life and enriches them nutritionally so the meat, milk, and eggs they give are the best quality, too.

Fat

I am very pro-fat. Depending on the headline at any given moment, this can seem like a solid or crazy statement to make. Like hemlines and hot vacation spots, it seems that opinions on fat change as frequently as fashion trends. One minute, everyone is scrambling to stock up on the latest low-fat, no-fat processed substitutes crowding the supermarket shelves; in the next instant, headlines read, "Butter Is Back!" But good food isn't a fad, and that goes for fat, too.

A drizzle of bacon fat, a schmear of schmaltz, some snowy white lard cut into pastry dough . . . cooks have long used the fat rendered from their cooking or gleaned from butchering as a secret ingredient in their best recipes. Today, many cooks still swear by the benefits and flavor of animal fat. *Lardo,* the Italian term for cured fatback, is considered a delicacy and in recent years has popped up on some of the toniest menus. Bakers are returning to rendered leaf lard for the flakiest piecrusts.

Animal fat used to be the cooking oil of choice. Good-quality fat provides great flavor to dishes—much more so than denatured, highly processed oils that have become popular in modern diets. Although it may seem counterintuitive to our modern sensibilities, foods fried in animal fat actually take up less of the oil than foods fried in the innocuous sounding but heavily refined "vegetable" oil (a.k.a. soybean oil).

Good fat comes from good animals. If you look at two steaks, side by side, the difference between a grass-fed animal and one raised on an artificial diet of grains and supplements is clear. The fat of the grass-fed animal is pearly and has a distinctive creamy yellow hue. It gets its color from the beta-carotene in the grass that it eats. That of the factory-raised animal is stark white and chalky, with none of the buttery tint encouraged by a field-based diet. Studies have shown that good-quality animal fats are high in essential fatty acids, such as omega-3s, that are present in cold-water fish, walnuts, and flaxseeds and have shown to have tremendous health benefits.

In many cases, fat is a "free" bonus gift that comes with your home cooking. Skimmed from the stockpot, drained from the pan, spooned from the roaster—it's not hard to come by. Even the prized leaf lard (the pork fat surrounding the kidneys), which is rendered and worked into the flakiest pastry dough, can be procured from your butcher for very little investment. Chicken fat, too. Good news—the proliferation of quality butchers and direct-from-farmer sourcing has made fat from well-raised animals increasingly available. And it will enrich the flavor of any recipe in which you use it. Tasty, good for you, and economical—call me crazy but fat sounds pretty fabulous.

HOW TO RENDER FAT

To get raw fat ready for your recipe, first it needs to be rendered—cooked slowly to release any meat or tissue from the fat, strained, and cooled. The result is creamy, silky fat that has the texture and versatility of butter. Leaf lard is the fat most often used for cooking. However, you can use fat trimmings from any cut of meat and the fat from fowl such as chicken, duck, and turkey as well. Here's a template to get you going.

Makes about 1 pint rendered lard from every pound of solid fat

2 pounds leaf lard or other fat or trimmings

½ cup water

➡ Chill the fat overnight so that it is easy to cut. Grind the fat in a meat grinder or food processor or cut it into small dice. Place the fat and ½ cup of water in an uncovered Dutch oven and heat over low heat for 3 to 4 hours, until the water has evaporated, the fat has melted, and any meat or skin has browned. Strain through a double thickness of cheesecloth to separate the liquid fat from the browned bits (see box). Pour the fat into heatproof jars or loaf pans lined with parchment, if you would like to have sliceable slabs. Allow to cool to room temperature and store in the refrigerator for 3 months or freeze for up to 1 year.

➡ continues

EAT IT UP! CRACKLINGS

The browned bits—called cracklings when you're rendering pork—are delicious and I have a hard time not simply gobbling them all up on the spot as a gift for the cook. If you have more willpower than I, you can use them in a variety of dishes. Their crunch and meaty flavor is a welcome addition to any salad where they bring the same satisfying bite as crumbled bacon. Use them as a garnish for soup, sprinkled on at the last instant before serving so they maintain their delightfully brittle texture. You can bake them into corn bread, throw them in a pot of braising greens, or sprinkle them on roasted vegetables. Cracklings are best straight off the heat but can be cooled, covered, and refrigerated for 3 to 4 days or frozen in an airtight container for up to 2 months. You can refresh some of their crispness, though not all of it, by reheating them in a dry pan over medium heat until they sizzle or popping them in a 325°F oven for 5 to 10 minutes.

HOW TO RENDER FAT continued

VARIATION: SCHMALTZ

To make schmaltz, the traditional chicken fat spread popular in Jewish cuisine; follow the recipe for rendering fat, substituting chicken fat and skin for the leaf lard. Cut the skin and fat into thin strips and render as directed, reducing the cooking time to about an hour. In the last half-hour of rendering, add a finely diced onion to the pot (make sure the fat is on very low heat, or it will sputter and burn). Strain, cool, and store as directed, enjoying the cracklings and fried onions (called *gribenes*) as a separate treat.

Schmaltz Thickener

Beurre manie, French for "kneaded butter," is a chef's trick for thickening sauces and gravies. Traditionally, equal parts of softened butter and flour are blended with a fork and added, a bit at a time to a too-thin sauce. You can make a similar product out of the schmaltz by whisking flour into a portion of the cooled but not hardened schmaltz before refrigerating for up to 7 days or freezing for up to 6 months. Alternatively, you can return a small amount of the schmaltz to a small skillet, whisk in the flour, and sauté until golden for a make-ahead roux, which can also be cooled, covered, and refrigerated for up to 7 days or frozen for up to 6 months.

Lard Dough

Lard makes for a phenomenal crust—tender with big, fish-scale flakes. You can use this crust for baking blue ribbon–worthy pies. It's also tops for empanadas, pasties, and other hand pies, wrapping Wellingtons, making quiche—really anywhere that a classic pastry crust is called for.

This recipe uses a combination of lard and butter: lard enables the texture; butter brings the flavor. For the best texture, make sure that both fats are well chilled before making the dough. I recommend popping them in the freezer for a few minutes after you've cut them into cubes, to make sure they're extra chilly. If it's a hot day, you might consider popping the flour and even your mixing bowl in the freezer for a few minutes as well, so they don't heat up your fat during blending.

Makes enough for two 9-inch piecrusts

2¼ cups all-purpose flour, frozen for 15 minutes

½ teaspoon kosher salt

8 tablespoons (1 stick) cold unsalted butter, cut into ½-inch pieces and frozen for 15 minutes

½ cup cold rendered leaf lard, cut into ½-inch pieces and frozen for 15 minutes

¼ to ½ cup ice water

➡ In a large bowl or a food processor, blend the flour and salt together. Add the butter and lard and cut together with two knives or a pastry blender until the fat is in pea-size lumps and the flour looks like damp sand. If you are using a food processor, pulse several times, scrape down the sides, and pulse again, repeating until you reach the desired texture. Using your knives or pastry blender or by pulsing the processor, incorporate the ice water 2 tablespoons at a time until the dough just comes together. Do not overwork the dough or it will be tough. Divide the dough in half, pat into disks, wrap in plastic or waxed paper, and refrigerate for at least 1 hour and up to 1 day. Proceed with your recipe. The dough can also be well wrapped and frozen for up to 6 months. Defrost in the fridge before using.

HOW TO PURIFY DRIPPINGS

Another excellent way to stock up on great animal fat is to save up your drippings. Fat from the skillet (such as bacon fat) or from a roasting pan (particularly roast duck and goose, which both throw off copious amounts of fat) bring great flavor and texture to many dishes. If you are going to use the drippings right away, you can just spoon them directly out of the pan and proceed with your recipe. But if you are going to store the drippings, it's best to make sure that you remove impurities to keep them from developing off flavors or spoiling.

METHOD 1

➡ This method is so easy and it's ideal for a small amount of drippings. Simply lay a paper towel over a heatproof jar, such as a canning jar, placed on a tea towel (the tea towel prevents thermal shock from the cold counter, which could break the glass). Press the center of the paper towel into the jar slightly to make a sort of cone shape. Slowly pour the hot drippings through the towel and into the jar. The paper towel will filter out all the impurities, leaving just the clean, pure oil in the jar. Allow to cool, cover, and refrigerate for 3 months or freeze for up to 1 year.

METHOD 2

➡ This method is perfect for dealing with large amount of drippings, such as the rivers of golden goodness that you will get from roasting a duck or goose. Pour the drippings into a medium-size saucepan. Add 2 cups of water and bring to a simmer over medium heat. Remove from the heat and allow to cool to room temperature. Place the entire saucepan in the refrigerator and chill overnight. All the impurities will sink to the bottom of the pan as the fat floats to the top. Remove the pan from the refrigerator. Run a knife around the inside of the pan to release the now solidified cap of fat. Pat it dry, allow it to slightly soften at room temperature, then press into ramekins or jars for storage. Cover and refrigerate for 3 months or freeze for up to 1 year.

Duck Fat Potatoes

This recipe is a family favorite. Popular in Britain and a staple at my English in-laws' holiday table, these potatoes are light and fluffy inside with a shatteringly crisp exterior. I have tried to make them with commercial oils and they never come out the same—it's the duck fat that gives them their brilliant crunch. We always have to roast a duck a week before Christmas, so I can make this special dish—and it's totally worth it!

You want a nice, medium-starch potato here—russets will fall apart and very waxy potatoes won't give you the crumble you need on the outside that becomes the crust. In the supermarket, look for "all-purpose" potatoes and if you are at the farmers' market, ask your grower for a recommendation.

Makes 4 servings, can be doubled

2 pounds all-purpose/medium-starch potatoes, peeled and cut into 2-inch pieces

    (see pages 84–87 for eating up potato peels)

Salt

¼ cup purified duck fat

Rosemary or thyme sprigs (optional)

- ➡ Preheat the oven to 375°F and place a large roasting pan in it.
- ➡ Place the potatoes in a large pot and cover with water by 2 inches. Add a handful or two of salt to the water (it should be as salty as seawater). Bring the potatoes to a boil over medium-high heat. Lower the heat and simmer just until the outsides begin to soften, about 10 minutes.
- ➡ While the potatoes are cooking, add the fat to the heating roasting pan. Drain the potatoes thoroughly in a colander. Return them to the pot, cover, and shake the pot vigorously to rough up the exterior of the potatoes. Carefully remove the pan of preheated fat from the oven. Dump the potatoes into the hot fat all at once. Toss them with a spatula to coat. Quickly sprinkle with salt and return them to the oven. Roast for 30 minutes.
- ➡ Remove the pan from the oven and use a sturdy spatula to turn the potatoes and scrape any browned bits from the bottom of the pan. Strew the herb sprigs, if using, on top of the potatoes and return them to the oven for 20 to 30 minutes more. Remove from the oven, adjust the seasoning, and serve immediately.

Yorkshire Pudding

Not a pudding at all, more like a puff. A delicious, crispy outside, chewy inside, popover sizzled in the fat from your Sunday roast. "Yorkshire pud" is a staple of the English table. So good, so easy. You can make the batter well in advance and then just bake them off while your roast rests. The only trick is to work quickly, getting the batter into the preheated fat lickety-split.

Yorkshire puds are so delicious, I'm surprised that they haven't jumped the pond. Maybe if we cooked more Sunday roasts, they would. I think my kids would lead the campaign for it. They love these popovers and gobble them up whenever I put together a batch. And gobble them up you must, as they are best piping hot, straight out of the oven.

Makes 1 dozen popovers, serving 6 or 2 very greedy children

4 large eggs

1½ cups whole milk

½ teaspoon salt

1¼ cups all-purpose flour

¼ cup beef drippings

➡ Combine the eggs, milk, and salt in a blender and puree until smooth. Add the flour and blend until smooth. Refrigerate for at least 4 hours and up to 2 days.

➡ Preheat the oven to 425°F. Place a popover pan or muffin tin on the top rack to preheat. Remove the pan from the oven and quickly add a teaspoon of fat to each cup. Return the pan to the oven to get the fat very hot, about 5 minutes. Pull the pan out of the oven and quickly divide the batter among the cups, filling each of them about three-quarters full. Immediately return the pan to the oven. The puddings will sizzle and rise. Bake until golden brown, 15 to 20 minutes. Serve immediately.

Giblets

Sounds cute, doesn't it? "Giblets" could be your puppy's name, it's so adorable. It's a great little twist of marketing. Giblets are actually the offal of fowl. When you purchase a whole bird, the giblets are what are in the little bag, usually accompanied by the neck.

As when shopping for any organ meat, it's important to make sure that those bits come from a well-raised animal. The organs are the plumbing of a beast—the filters, pumps, and processors. Often times, they are the first line of defense between the animal and its environment. As such, they absorb and process many of the toxins that an animal encounters in its life. So, the better the conditions in which the animal was raised, the better its feed, the better quality of the offal it provides. Make sure that the giblets for your recipes come from a trusted farmer, butcher, or are certified organic, for the best results.

WHAT'S IN THE BAG?

Probably the least favorite part of roasting a bird for many home cooks is reaching into the cavity to remove "the bag." Many simply chuck it in the garbage without giving it a second glance. Others open it up, turn up their nose, and then chuck it. What is that small collection of grizzly bits, anyway? You may find one or more of the following items:

The neck—technically this is not a giblet, but it is often included in the bag or alongside the bag. It looks pretty much like what it is, long, bony, skinned, and usually curved.

The gizzard—this is the part of the bird's digestive system that grinds up grain and other hard materials. It is firm, often has two lobes connected by some tissue, and is covered by a tough membrane.

The heart—this is small, firm, and looks somewhat like an acorn in its size and shape. If you've seen other animal hearts, this looks like a mini-version of the organ.

The kidneys—not always found in the bag, these are small, very dark, and soft.

The liver—medium brown, very soft, they feel almost liquid in the hand.

If you've never cooked with these items before, they can look a little intimidating and they're so small you may not think they are worth the trouble. But these little tidbits have a lot of flavor. At the very least, they are worth throwing into your stockpot—except for the liver, which can impart a bitter flavor when prepared in this way. Livers are best left to their own special treatment (see page 126).

If you're not going to use the giblets right away, you can cover and refrigerate them but for no longer than a day or two as they're quite perishable. For longer storage, wrap well and freeze for up to 3 months.

Giblet Gravy

This is the gravy I make every Thanksgiving. It has a deep, rich, very "turkey" flavor. I start with a large batch of Brown Chicken Stock (page 143) to get a head start and to ensure that we have lots of gravy—you'll be amazed at how quickly it goes. I strain out my giblets, so my gravy is silky smooth, but some eaters prefer to chop them up and stir them back into the gravy. Your call.

This recipe assumes that you are roasting a turkey and calls for all the good drippings in the roasting pan. You could also use the same recipe for roast chicken with gravy, adjusting the yield to suit the size of your crowd.

Makes about 1½ quarts, serving 14 to 16

Contents of the giblet bag (such as the neck, heart, gizzard, and/or kidneys), except the liver

Salt

2 tablespoons neutral oil, such as organic canola

1 quart Brown Chicken Stock (page 143)

½ cup drippings from roasted turkey

1 shallot, finely minced

1 tablespoon chopped fresh herbs, such as sage or thyme (optional)

½ cup all-purpose flour

1 cup dry white wine

➡ Pat the giblets dry and sprinkle with salt. In a 3- to 4-quart saucepan, sauté the giblets in the oil over medium heat until well browned, about 10 minutes, turning halfway through to ensure even cooking. Cover with 2 quarts of cold water and bring to a simmer. Lower the heat and simmer gently while your turkey roasts, at least 2 hours (top up with cold water if the water level threatens to recede below the giblets). Remove from the heat and strain through a fine-mesh sieve. You should have about 1 quart of giblet stock. Transfer this stock back to the saucepan, add the Brown Chicken Stock, and keep warm over low heat. When the giblets are cool enough to handle, you can mince the organs and pull the meat off the neck to add back into your finished gravy or use in another recipe, such as the Giblet Stuffing (page 124).

➡ continues

GIBLET GRAVY *continued*

➡ Remove your roasting bird from the oven and set it aside to rest while you make the gravy. Pour off the drippings from the pan into a heatproof bowl or measuring cup. Give the fat a few minutes to separate out from the drippings and rise to the top. Spoon about ¼ cup of the clear fat back into the roasting pan, reserving the remaining drippings. (If more fat rises above the drippings, spoon it off and reserve for another use.) Set the pan over one or two burners on medium-low heat. Add the minced shallot to the pan along with the herbs, if using, and sauté until translucent, 2 to 3 minutes. Add the flour and whisk it into the fat and shallots in the roasting pan. It will form a paste. Add the wine and whisk with the flour paste until smooth. Pour reserved drippings back into the pan and whisk to combine. Slowly add the stock mixture, whisking all the while to ensure a smooth gravy. Simmer for 5 minutes to thicken. At this point you can strain out the shallot for a perfectly smooth gravy, add the chopped giblets and neck meat for a more rustic gravy, or leave it as is. Adjust the seasonings. Transfer to a gravy boat or insulated carafe, and serve.

➡ Leftover gravy keeps, cooled, covered, and refrigerated, for 3 to 5 days. Thin with water, if necessary, when reheating.

Giblet Stuffing

The flavorful stock and tasty bits of simmered giblets make this stuffing stand out. Although it's great alongside a roast bird, you can save your giblets in the freezer and make it anytime. If you're lucky enough to have some left over, press it into patties and sauté to rewarm—crispy on the outside and soft and pillowy inside. They're so satisfying topped with a fried egg for breakfast or with a salad of bitter greens for lunch.

The recipe might seem like a lot of work, but it can be spread out over a few days. The giblet stock can be made several days ahead, covered, and refrigerated with the accompanying neck meat and diced giblets also well covered and refrigerated. The bread can be toasted up to 2 days ahead; just make sure to toast it thoroughly and cool it completely before sealing away in an airtight container. The aromatic vegetables can be made ahead as well. All the components come together quite quickly with those steps out of the way.

Makes 8 to 10 servings

Contents of the giblet bag (such as the neck, heart, gizzard, and kidneys), except the liver

Salt

2 tablespoons neutral oil, such as organic canola

1 (16-ounce) loaf Italian bread, cut into 1-inch cubes (about 8 cups)

2 tablespoons olive oil

1 teaspoon dried thyme

Salt and freshly ground black pepper

2 tablespoons unsalted butter

1 onion, diced

3 celery stalks, diced

2 garlic cloves, minced

1 cup white wine

1 large egg, beaten

2 ounces Parmigiano-Reggiano cheese, grated (about ½ cup)

¼ cup pine nuts (also called pignoli) (optional)

½ cup finely minced fresh parsley

➡ *continues*

Make the Stock (can be done 3 to 4 days ahead)

➥ Pat the giblets dry and sprinkle with salt. In a 3- to 4-quart saucepan, sauté the giblets in the oil over medium heat until well browned, about 10 minutes, turning halfway through to ensure even cooking. Cover with 2 quarts of cold water and bring to a simmer. Lower the heat and simmer gently, at least 2 hours (top up with cold water if the water level threatens to recede below the giblets). Remove from the heat and strain through a fine-mesh sieve. Return the stock to the pot and simmer over medium heat until reduced to 2 cups. Allow to cool slightly before proceeding with the recipe, or cool completely, cover, and refrigerate for up to 4 days. When cool enough to handle, pull the meat from the neck, finely dice it and the giblets, cover, and refrigerate if not using immediately and for no more than 3 to 4 days.

Toast the Bread (can be done while the stock is simmering or up to 2 days ahead)

➥ Preheat the oven to 300°F. Arrange the bread cubes on a rimmed cookie sheet. Drizzle with the olive oil, sprinkle with the thyme, and season with salt and pepper. Toss to combine. Toast in the oven until lightly browned and dried through, about 20 minutes, turning frequently to avoid burning. Use immediately or cool and store in an airtight container for up to 2 days.

Prepare the Vegetables (can be done while the stock is simmering and the bread is toasting or up to 8 hours ahead, refrigerate if making more than 2 hours ahead)

➥ Sauté the onion and the celery in the butter in a medium-size sauté pan over medium heat until translucent, 3 to 5 minutes. Add the garlic and sauté until fragrant, about 1 minute. Add the wine and simmer until reduced by half. Remove from the heat and allow to cool to room temperature if proceeding with the recipe, or cool, cover, and refrigerate for up to 8 hours.

Make the Stuffing (assemble and pop into the oven an hour before dinner)

➥ Preheat the oven to 350°F. Butter a 4-quart casserole dish and set it aside. In a large bowl, whisk together the cooled vegetable mixture, egg, and giblet stock. Add the toasted bread cubes and toss to allow the bread to soak up the liquid. Add the cheese, nuts, if using, parsley, and reserved neck meat and giblets and toss to combine. Transfer to the casserole dish and cover with foil. Bake for 20 minutes. Remove the foil and bake until the top is browned, an additional 20 to 30 minutes. Serve immediately. Leftovers keep, cooled, covered, and refrigerated, for 3 to 5 days.

Livers

Chicken livers. I don't know about you, but this is one ingredient that just sounds so '70s to me. Very "wide lapel and maxi dress" cocktail party. Livers were all the rage then and, with nose-to-tail cooking gaining popularity, they are seeing their heyday again.

You can buy chicken livers from your butcher expressly for these recipes. Cook them quickly, within one or two days of purchase. Or you can save them up from your giblet bag in a little airtight container in the freezer for three to four months, until you have enough livers for the recipe, and defrost before proceeding. Then try one of these quick, retro cool concoctions and it's all groovy, baby.

Bacon-Wrapped Chicken Livers

Also called rumaki, these little tidbits were all the rage back in the day. They were popular at the hot spot Trader Vic's, where their exotic soy sauce glaze fit right in with the tikki bar culture. Enjoy them with a mai tai for the ultimate throwback experience.

The crisp bacon, tender liver, and crunchy water chestnut make for a nicely varied texture combination. The slightly gamey flavor of the liver is cherished by many, but not all. So, when making these for company, you might want to make a few extra, without the livers. Bacon-wrapped water chestnuts are still tasty. Dates work well, too.

Makes 12 wrapped livers

2 tablespoons soy sauce

2 tablespoons pure maple syrup

12 chicken livers

12 water chestnut halves, or 6 water chestnuts cut in half equatorially

6 strips bacon, halved crosswise

➡ Preheat the oven to 400°F. Soak twelve wooden skewers in water for 30 minutes as the oven heats.

➡ Combine the soy sauce and maple syrup in a small bowl and stir to blend. Set aside.

➡ Wrap a chicken liver around a water chestnut half. Wrap that with half a strip of bacon and pierce with a skewer to secure. Repeat with remaining chicken livers.

➡ Place the skewers on a rimmed cookie sheet. Use a pastry brush to brush the soy sauce mixture on the threaded livers. Bake until the bacon is crispy and the livers are cooked through, about 20 minutes. Serve immediately.

Sautéed Chicken Livers

Eat your liver! It's a time-honored battle cry of mothers trying to get the nutritive benefits of liver into their kids' diets. Some people love it for its distinct flavor and healthful properties—liver is famously rich in iron and is often fed to expectant and nursing mothers for its nutrient-dense properties. Others find its slightly bitter taste off-putting. This recipe is so luxurious and decadent, you won't need any cajoling. Even liver haters will succumb to the divine cream and brandy sauce. Elegant and classic, serve it as a first course for your next gathering.

Makes 4 servings

1 pound chicken livers

2 tablespoons unsalted butter

1 onion, chopped

Salt and freshly ground black pepper

1 garlic clove, minced

¼ cup brandy

½ cup heavy cream

Toast points

➡ Separate the chicken livers into lobes, if necessary, and pat dry. Sauté the livers in the butter in a large sauté pan until browned and just cooked through, about 5 minutes. Use a slotted spoon to remove them from the pan. Add the onion to the pan, season with salt and pepper, and sauté until translucent, 3 to 5 minutes. Add the garlic and sauté until fragrant, about a minute. Add the brandy and simmer until reduced and syrupy, about 3 minutes. (Be careful adding liquor to a hot pot. Always have a pot lid nearby in case the brandy flames.) Whisk in the cream and simmer until thickened, about 2 minutes. Return the livers to the pan and simmer gently until heated through, 1 to 2 minutes. Adjust the seasoning and serve immediately, garnished with toast points.

The Beauty of Bones

Bones, they're not just for dogs anymore. Turns out Fido might be on to something. Bones are rich in vitamins, minerals, and viscous gelatin that are great to have in our diet. The curative powers of chicken soup may be all in the bones used to make the stock. The slow simmering of bone broths and braises coaxes all the essential elements out of the bones and into the liquid of the recipe so that we can reap their benefits.

As with other parts such as fat and organs, when buying bones it is particularly important to source products from well-raised animals. Like organ meats, bones can leach and store toxins from the animals' environment, so be sure that the ingredients in your bone recipes come from reputable farmers who adhere to sustainable practices. Time spent in the fresh air and sunshine, a high-quality/species-appropriate diet, and no prophylactic antibiotics or artificial hormones are a good start for farm animals and for us, too!

ANATOMY OF A BONE

Bones add a lot of flavor to the dish. Whether they're slow-roasted or quickly pan-seared, your recipes will benefit from being cooked on the bone. The skeletal framework holds the shape of the cut during cooking, making it much easier to handle in the pan and reducing shrinkage. Bones impart flavor and substance to any dish—from full crown roasts to small, bony fishes—releasing rich flavor and unctuous collagen as the meal is cooked.

Your recipe will determine the kind of bones you need. You can use most any bone to make stock—chicken, veal, and beef bones are the most popular. The silky marrow, considered a delicacy by many, is present in all bones but most abundant in the leg bones of ruminants, such as sheep and cows. Some cuts, such as shanks and ribs, are mostly bone with a small amount of meat attached. These are excellent for low and slow braising where the bone supports the dish with flavor and texture. The following recipes cover all these bone bases.

Braised Lamb Shanks

While this recipe is for lamb shanks, you can use the same technique for other big bony cuts, such as osso buco. Although it takes some time from start to finish, the majority of the cooking is unattended, so you get to just enjoy the perfume of the simmering pot while time does its magic. The long, lingering bath gives the bones the chance to give up all their flavor and gravy-thickening magic and makes the meat fall-off-the-bone tender. Serve this dish with something comforting and starchy, such as garlic mashed potatoes or polenta, which will soak up the sauce.

Makes 4 servings

4 lamb shanks

Salt

2 tablespoons neutral oil, such as organic canola

1 onion, diced

2 celery stalks, diced

2 carrots, diced

6 garlic cloves, whole

2 cups fruity red wine, such as Beaujolais

2 tablespoons tomato paste

2 cups Brown Chicken Stock (page 143)

1 teaspoon dried thyme

2 dried bay leaves

→ Pat the shanks dry and season well with salt. Heat the oil in a Dutch oven or other heavy-bottomed pot over medium heat until shimmering. Add the shanks and brown thoroughly, turning three times to brown all over, 15 to 20 minutes total. Remove the shanks from the pan and set aside.

→ *continues*

BRAISED LAMB SHANKS *continued*

→ Add the onion, celery, and carrots to the pan and sauté until the onion is translucent and the other vegetables have softened, 5 to 7 minutes. Add the garlic and sauté until fragrant, about a minute. Add the wine, paste, stock, thyme, and bay leaves and bring to a simmer, stirring occasionally to dissolve the tomato paste. Return the shanks to the pan. Cover, lower the heat to low, and gently simmer, partially covered, until the meat is nearly tender, about 1½ hours.

→ Remove from the heat. Strain the liquid through a fine-mesh sieve into a heatproof bowl. Set the strainer full of shanks and vegetables aside. Allow the liquid to settle for 15 minutes to allow the fat to rise to the top. Skim off as much fat as possible (see page 113 for ways to use up quality fat). Return the defatted liquid to the pan along with the shanks and vegetables. Return the heat to a simmer, leaving the pot uncovered. Continue to simmer until the meat is very tender, about an additional 30 minutes. Adjust the seasoning and serve or allow to cool, cover, and refrigerate for up to 3 days and reheat before serving.

Ham Hock Greens

Southerners have a way with greens, particularly low- and slow-braising greens like collards and mustards. The ham hock helps; it imparts deep flavor to the pot, particularly if it is a smoked ham hock. After stewing, the meat can be pulled off the bone and added to the dish or piled onto a nice, soft baguette for the ultimate sandwich.

When I am cooking up a mess of greens, I make a big pot. It's a great dish for entertaining—you can make it ahead and everyone loves it. They also keep and reheat beautifully, so any leftovers won't be left over for long.

Makes 12 servings

PREPPING COLLARDS

Staring down a pile of greens can be intimidating. Here's how to prep them. Wash your collards thoroughly. Working a leaf at a time (don't worry, it goes quickly), fold the leaf in half and use a paring knife to slice out the rib. Proceed with all the leaves, separating the leaves and stems. Chop the stems to desired length and set aside. Stack the de-ribbed leaves into piles of twelve. Roll the pile into a cigar shape and cut it into pieces of your desired width (anything from a fine ¼-inch chiffonade to 2-inch pieces). If you want square pieces instead of long strands, cut across the pile in the opposite direction.

1 large onion, diced

2 tablespoons olive oil

4 pounds collard greens, ribs removed and diced, leaves cut into 2-inch pieces (see inset on prepping collards)

2 garlic cloves, sliced

1 ham hock, preferably smoked

3 quarts Blonde Chicken Stock (page 142) or water

¼ cup soy sauce

1 cup white wine

¼ cup cider vinegar

Hot sauce, such as Crystal or Tabasco

Salt and freshly ground black pepper

➡ In a large Dutch oven or other heavy-bottomed pot, sauté the onion in the olive oil over medium heat until transparent, 5 to 7 minutes. Add the collard ribs and sauté until bright green, 5 to 7 minutes. Add the collard leaves and sauté until bright green, 7 to 10 minutes. Add the garlic, ham hock, stock, soy sauce, wine, vinegar, and a few good splashes of hot sauce. Bring to a boil. Lower the heat and simmer until the meat is falling off the bone and the collards are tender, 1½ to 2 hours. Remove from the heat. Remove the hock from the pot. When cool enough to handle, remove the meat from the bone. Shred and return the meat to the pot, if desired. Adjust the seasoning and serve. Keeps, cooled, covered, and refrigerated, for 3 to 5 days.

Bajan Pepper Pot

I had my first bowl of pepper pot on a family trip to Barbados. We went for Sunday meal at a local cafe that served a gorgeous spread of every Bajan delicacy, the centerpiece being the pepper pot—a rich stew studded with spices that made the whole room smell warm, welcoming, and decidedly exotic. Entire families filled their plates and then sat down to dig in, passing fidgety babies from lap to lap so everybody got a chance to tuck in to their good meal.

Pepper pot is traditionally made with several kinds of slow-stewing meats—beef, pork, and chicken are all fair game, so feel free to use a combination of whatever looks good in the market. I like oxtails and beef chuck for their hearty, deep flavor. Lighten up your plate by serving this stewed pot of meaty goodness with lighter sides that are heavy on the vegetables, such as the Quinoa Salad with Roots and Greens (page 26) or the Broccoli Slaw (page 37).

You can vary the amount of heat to your taste. The peppers cook for a long time, so don't be afraid of using at least one Scotch bonnet. The low and slow cooking is long enough to burn off the heat of this notoriously tongue-singeing chili, leaving behind the fruitiness of the pepper.

Makes 6 to 8 servings

2 pounds oxtails

Salt

¼ cup olive oil

2 quarts Beef or Veal Stock (page 140)

2 pounds beef chuck, cut into 2-inch cubes

2 onions, diced

4 garlic cloves, sliced

2 tablespoons minced fresh ginger

1 to 2 Scotch bonnet peppers, minced (use rubber gloves when mincing peppers
    and be sure to wash your cutting board thoroughly after use)

1 tablespoon ground allspice

½ teaspoon ground cloves

■ continues

BAJAN PEPPER POT *continued*

1 teaspoon dried thyme

Freshly ground black pepper

2 tablespoons molasses

→ Pat the oxtails dry and season with salt. In a Dutch oven or other heavy-bottomed pot, heat 2 tablespoons of the olive oil over medium heat until shimmering. Add the oxtails and sauté until browned, turning halfway through, for a total of about 10 minutes. Add the stock to the pot and bring to a simmer, scraping up the browned bits on the bottom of the pot. Lower the heat and simmer, partially covered, for 1 hour.

→ Meanwhile, brown the chuck. Pat the meat dry and season it well with salt. In a large sauté pan, heat the remaining 2 tablespoons of oil over medium heat until shimmering. Working in batches, if necessary, to avoid crowding the pan, brown the cubes, turning occasionally, for about 10 minutes and transfer to a bowl. Add the onions and sauté until translucent, 3 to 5 minutes. Add the garlic, ginger, and Scotch bonnet and sauté until fragrant, about 1 minute. Add the allspice, cloves, thyme, and black pepper to taste and sauté for 30 seconds. Add a ladleful of the oxtail liquid to deglaze the pan by bringing it to a simmer and scraping up all the browned bits on the bottom. Add this to the simmering oxtails along with the browned chuck and continue to simmer for 1 hour.

→ Strain the contents of the pot through a fine-mesh strainer set over a heatproof bowl. Set the strained meat and vegetables aside. Allow the liquid to settle for 10 to 15 minutes, to allow the fat to rise to the top. Spoon off as much fat as possible (see page 113 for tips on using up good fat). Return the defatted liquid to the pan and simmer until reduced by one third. Add the molasses and strained meat and vegetables to the pot and simmer for 20 to 30 minutes more, until the meat of the oxtails is falling off the bone and the chuck is fork-tender. Pepper pot can be served immediately but tastes even better cooled, covered, and refrigerated for at least 1 and up to 5 days. Can also be frozen for up to 3 months.

Roasted Bone Marrow on Toast

Bone marrow, the silky fat nestled in the core of a ruminant's leg bones, is a delicacy that comes in and out of fashion. It is vilified by some generations as too fatty, adored by others for its luxurious fattiness. It's long been a staple on European menus and pops up regularly in farm-to-table restaurants. Whether you are a die-hard fan or have never tried it, making marrowbones at home is an easy thing to do. You can serve the marrow along with toast points as an app, as I've done here, or work the buttery richness into other recipes, such as dumpling fillings, sauces, and gravies or as a mix-in that will bring your burger to the next level. Marrow spoons are long, thin scoops that allow you to get easy access to the good stuff. But if you don't have those, just dig in with a butter knife.

Makes 4 servings

8 marrowbones, 3 to 4 inches in length

4 pieces toast, or a toasted baguette torn into chunks

Kosher or sea salt

➡ Preheat the oven to 425°F. Arrange the bones, cut side down, on a sided cookie sheet or in a heat-proof pan. Roast for 20 to 25 minutes, until a skewer inserted into the marrow meets no resistance and the marrow is beginning to melt out of the bones a little bit. Serve immediately with toast points or bread and a little salt to sprinkle on top.

Braised Short Ribs with Chocolate

Short ribs are a magical cut of meat. Bone in, ribboned with good fat, and thickly cut, they make for the most satisfying knock-the-chill-off Sunday dinner. Along with some comforting sides they dazzle at the company's-come-for-dinner table. Short ribs, like many of the bone-centric cuts, behave best when slowly simmered, roasted, or stewed. Here, they are braised with warm spices and chocolate—not quite a mole, but not too far off, either. Use that as your launching point for sides—rice and beans if you're feeling casual, a sweet potato gratin if you want to dress it up. Make extra of everything because you are going to be sad when it's gone.

Makes 4 servings

4 pounds bone-in short ribs (cut parallel to the bone, not "flanken" style),
    cut into roughly 3-inch pieces

Salt

2 tablespoons neutral oil, such as organic canola

1 onion, diced

6 garlic cloves, peeled but left whole

2 teaspoons paprika

1 tablespoon ground coriander

1 tablespoon ground cumin

2 tablespoons unsweetened cocoa powder (preferably Dutch process)

2 cups canned whole tomatoes with their juices, preferably home-canned,
    pureed with an immersion blender

2 cups fruity red wine, such as Beaujolais

2 cups Brown Chicken Stock (page 143)

1 dried ancho chili, stemmed and seeded

Freshly ground black pepper

➡ continues

BRAISED SHORT RIBS WITH CHOCOLATE *continued*

➡ Pat the ribs dry and season them well with salt. In a large Dutch oven or other deep, heavy pot, heat the oil over medium heat until shimmering. Working in batches if necessary to avoid crowding the pan, brown the ribs on all sides, about 10 minutes total. Repeat with remaining ribs, transferring each batch to a bowl as they are browned. Spoon off all but 2 tablespoons of the rendered fat and reserve for another use (see page 113 for recipes using rendered beef fat).

➡ Add the onion and sauté until translucent, 3 to 5 minutes. Add the garlic and sauté for a minute or so more. Add the paprika, coriander, cumin, and cocoa powder and sauté for 30 seconds. Add the tomatoes and simmer until thickened slightly, 3 to 5 minutes, stirring occasionally to release the browned bits from the bottom of the pan. Add the wine and simmer for 5 minutes. Add the stock, chili, and pepper to taste and bring to a simmer. Return the ribs to the pot, cover, lower the heat, and simmer gently for 1½ to 2 hours, until the meat is nearly fork-tender.

➡ Using tongs, gently remove the ribs from the pot. Use a ladle to defat the braising liquid (see page 113 for using up beef fat). Using an immersion blender, puree the contents of the pot (if you like less heat, remove the ancho before pureeing). Return the ribs to the pot and continue to gently simmer for 30 to 45 minutes, until the meat threatens to fall off the bone. (You can add a splash of water to the sauce if it is so thick that it threatens to scorch.) Remove from the heat and serve or cool and refrigerate, covered, for up to 2 days. Reheat gently before serving.

Broth/Stock/Bone Broth

Broth, stock, and bone broth are three variations of the same thing—bones simmered in water. Broth is the lightest, simmering for only an hour or two. Stock simmers a little longer—three to four hours. Bone broth is the same combination: bones + water + time, just with more time—sometimes 24 hours or longer. For simplicity's sake, let's use the typical term you'd hear in a professional kitchen, *stock*, to talk about the many benefits of this good-cooking staple.

Stock will elevate the quality of any dish in which you use it. It doesn't just bring liquid to your recipes; stock also brings body. The slow simmering that goes into making a good stock dissolves a number of elements in the bones that are inaccessible through any other cooking method. Collagen and cartilage liquefy into the stock, giving it a viscosity that fills out a recipe with an almost voluptuous quality. Gravies are luscious; soups are rich, not watery; and stews take on an unctuous mouthfeel. The longer you simmer your stock, the more collagen dissolves in the water and the more gelatinous it becomes; so much so that when chilled, you will be able to slice it into cubes (the secret to making soup dumplings, in fact, is to encase a cube of chilled stock in each wrapper—it melts when the dumpling hits the heat of the pan and when you bite it—soup!).

The dissolved collagen, cartilage, and other trace vitamins and minerals found in slowly simmered stock are also reported to be terrific for you. Stock advocates, such as Sally Fallon Morrell, author of *Nourishing Broth*, claim that the stuff can not only give you shiny hair and strong nails but also alleviate joint pain and inflammation, boost cell repair, and restore you with its antiaging properties. This may sound like a lot to lay on a bowl of soup, but although science is just beginning to study the pros of including stock in one's diet, ancient wisdom has long supported its benefits. Across cultures, stock is taken as both a preventative and a cure. Asian cuisine relies heavily on simmered stocks as part of the daily diet. "Jewish penicillin," a.k.a. chicken soup, is commonly reached for to soothe coughs and colds. Stock feels good in our body—and if my body thinks it's good for me, I tend to agree.

And stock tastes good. Almost primal-good. How often is that first sip of soup followed by an unbidden "Mmmmmm?" That num-num sound is proof. Not just to our intellectual eating self that can tally up the quantitative nutrition of stock; or the "food groupie" self that would be willing to wait in line for the next molecular gastronomy concoction. That sound is the voice of our tiny reptile brain being deeply satisfied. That's what stock will get you.

Following are the master recipes for three kinds of stock—Beef or Veal, Blonde Chicken (from raw bones), and Brown Chicken (from roasted bones). You can use these as templates for all stocks—turkey, duck, pork. Whatever kind of stock you are making, the goal is flavorful liquid that is crystal clear. To avoid cloudy stock, follow these golden rules:

—Never boil
—Never stir
—Never cover

Beef or Veal Stock

Roasted bones are the key to good beef and veal stock. Without this extra dose of heat, these stocks can taste a tad off with a sort of metallic taste. A good pass through a hot oven also gives the stock the rich, round flavors that only roasting can bring. Deglazing the pan with a little bit of wine to dissolve the browned, caramelized juices off the bottom of the pan, also known as the *fond*, ensures that you get every last lick of your dinner's goodness. And, bonus, the acid and alcohol in the vino will free some of the flavor compounds that aren't water-soluble. The long simmer on the stove burns off all the alcohol, leaving great taste behind without any threat of a buzz-inducing bowl of soup.

You can use this template for both beef and veal stocks. Make your stock with just bones and water or add a few roasted vegetables, as I've done here, to build layers of flavor. If using vegetables, you can roast them with the bones, but add them to the pot toward the end of cooking—vegetables simmered for too long tend to go bitter.

Makes about 3 quarts stock

5 pounds beef or veal bones (any bones will do, but knuckle bones have an abundance of gelatin that will add great body to your stock)

¼ cup neutral oil, such as organic canola

Salt

2 carrots (optional)

1 celery stalk (optional)

2 onions, halved but not peeled (optional)

1 head of garlic, cut in half equatorially (optional)

2 cups dry white wine, such as sauvignon blanc

1 bay leaf

½ teaspoon dried thyme

6 peppercorns

● *continues*

➡ Preheat the oven to 400°F. Arrange the bones in a single layer in one or two large roasting pans—be sure to avoid crowding. Rub the oil into the bones to coat evenly. Sprinkle generously with salt. Place in the oven and roast until well browned, about 1 hour to 1 hour 15 minutes. If using vegetables, add them to the pan for the last 45 minutes of roasting.

➡ Remove the pan from the oven. Remove the vegetables and set aside. Transfer the browned bones to a large stockpot and set aside. Deglaze the roasting pan by placing it over two burners over medium heat. When the drippings begin to sizzle, add the wine all at once to the pan (be careful, the liquid will hiss and spit). Use a whisk to scrape up all the browned bits on the bottom of the pan and blend them into the simmering wine. Add this liquid to the stockpot along with the bay leaf, thyme, and peppercorns.

➡ Cover the bones by 2 inches with cold water, about 1 gallon, and place over medium heat and bring to a simmer. Lower the heat and gently simmer for at least 2 hours and up to 6. Add the vegetables in the last 2 hours of cooking (refrigerate the vegetables if the time between roasting and adding to the pot exceeds 2 hours).

➡ Strain the stock through a fine-mesh sieve, chinois, or colander lined with a double thickness of cheesecloth into a heatproof bowl. Allow to cool to room temperature, then refrigerate until completely cooled and the fat has solidified on the top of the stock. Remove the solidified cap of fat and reserve for another use (see page 113 for tips on using up quality fat). The stock keeps refrigerated for 5 days or frozen for up to 6 months, or will be shelf stable for up to a year if pressure canned.

Blonde Chicken Stock

Blonde chicken stock, so called because it is made from raw rather than roasted bones, is light in flavor and color and brings a savory note to the dish that doesn't compete with other ingredients. This stock is great to use in recipes where you want more flavor, but not necessarily more chicken flavor. It's my go-to in dishes that spotlight vegetables, such as something like pea soup or butternut squash risotto, where a little umami is welcome but you want the clear, clean flavor of the plant to really shine. You can add aromatic vegetables in the last two hours of cooking, if you like. But more often than not, I make this stock out of just bones and water.

Makes about 3 quarts stock

4 pounds chicken bones (such as necks, backs, wings, and feet)

Salt

1 carrot (optional)

1 celery stalk (optional)

1 garlic clove, unpeeled (optional)

½ onion, ½ cup leek greens, or 1 shallot (optional)

➡ Place the bones in a large stockpot, add a generous pinch of salt and cover with water by 2 inches (about 1 gallon). Place over medium heat and bring to a simmer, being careful not to boil. Lower the heat and gently simmer for at least 2 hours and up to 6, adding the vegetables, if using, in the last 2 hours of simmering.

➡ Strain the stock through a fine-mesh sieve, chinois, or colander lined with a double thickness of cheesecloth into a heatproof bowl. Discard the bones. Allow to cool to room temperature, then refrigerate until completely cooled and the fat has solidified on the top of the stock. Remove the solidified cap of fat and reserve for another use (see page 113 for tips on using up quality fat). The stock keeps refrigerated for 5 days or frozen for up to 6 months, or will be shelf stable for up to a year if pressure canned.

Brown Chicken Stock

This is the stock I make most often. The bones are roasted before simmering to bring out their flavor, caramelize the roasting juices, and deepen the taste and color of the stock. I don't use any aromatics in this stock and I simmer it for a long time, often overnight, so it's really meaty tasting, robust, and gelatinous. You can tell that your bones have given their all in this recipe—they snap like twigs by the end of it. Everything that's good about them goes right into the pot.

Makes about 1 gallon stock

5 pounds chicken bones (such as backs, necks, wings, and at least a few feet for their
    abundance of gelatin)

2 tablespoons neutral oil, such as organic canola

Salt

1 cup dry white wine, such as sauvignon blanc, or water

- Preheat the oven to 400°F. Place the bones in a large roasting pan, drizzle them with the oil, and rub it in to make sure all is thoroughly coated. Season generously with salt. Roast until the bones are browned and the pan juices are sticky and dark brown, about 1 hour to an hour and a half. Transfer the bones to a large stockpot and set aside. Place the roaster over two burners set over medium heat. Add the wine to deglaze the pan, using a whisk to scrape up the brown *fond* on the bottom and blend it into the liquid. Add the deglazing liquid to the pot. Cover with cold water by 2 inches (about 5 quarts). Set the stockpot over medium heat and bring to a simmer—do not boil. Lower the heat to low and gently simmer for at least 4 and up to 12 hours.
- Strain the stock through a fine-mesh sieve, chinois, or colander lined with a double thickness of cheesecloth into a heatproof bowl. Discard the bones. Allow to cool to room temperature, then refrigerate until completely cooled and the fat has solidified on the top of the stock. Remove the solidified cap of fat and reserve for another use (see page 113 for tips on using up quality fat). The stock keeps refrigerated for 5 days or frozen for up to 6 months, or will be shelf stable for up to a year if pressure canned.

How to Butcher a Chicken

If there is one kitchen skill that I could teach home cooks, it is how to break down a chicken. It is the single most useful, cost-saving, flavor-increasing technique in the home cooking playbook. You will pay less for your poultry; whole chickens are infinitely less expensive than boneless and even bone-in breasts and thighs as well. Plus, break down your own bird and you get the bonus of the wings, backs, and neck to turn into stock. It's like getting a free pot of soup with every bird. A whole chicken also gives you more information about the bird. Lack of bruising or broken wings or legs lets you know that the bird was in good shape on the farm. And once you master this technique, carving the Thanksgiving bird will be a cinch.

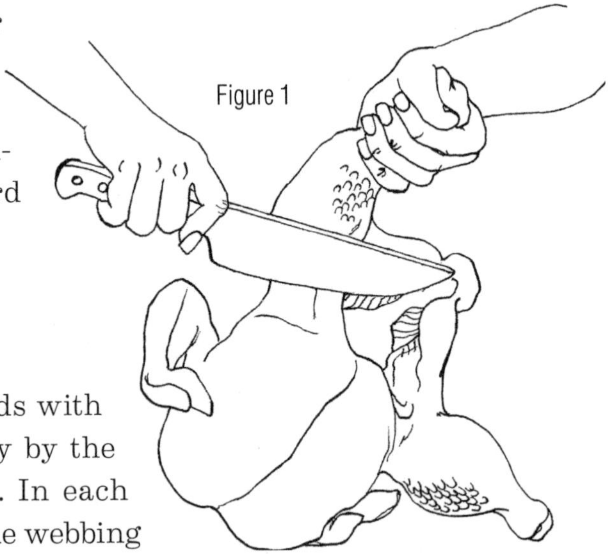

Figure 1

STEP 1: REMOVE THE LEGS/THIGHS

To remove a leg and thigh, shake hands with your chicken. Grab the chicken firmly by the drumstick and lift up the whole bird. In each joint, there is a web of skin, similar to the webbing between your thumb and index finger. Locate the webbing between the thigh and the body and slice through it perpendicularly, being careful not to cut all the way through to the muscle (Figure 1). Continue to cut a wide circle around the joint with your knife, being sure to cut out the "oyster," the generous mouthful of meat at the back of the hip joint (Figure 2).

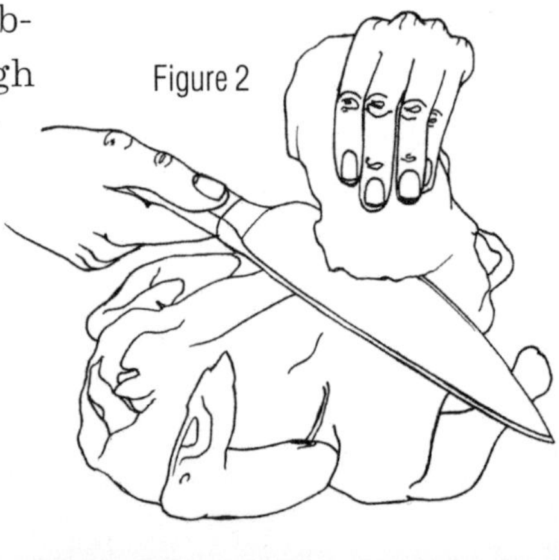

Figure 2

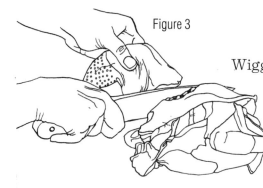

Figure 3

Wiggle your knife in between the thigh joint and the body and slice through to separate the thigh and leg from the body. Repeat on the other side (Figure 3).

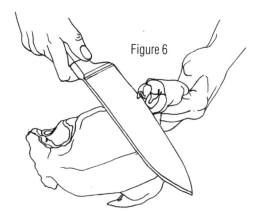

Figure 4

To separate the leg from the thigh, look again for the webbing at the joint between the two. Slice through that webbing perpendicularly, on through the joint, and you will be rewarded with two pieces. On now to leg two, following the same process (Figure 4).

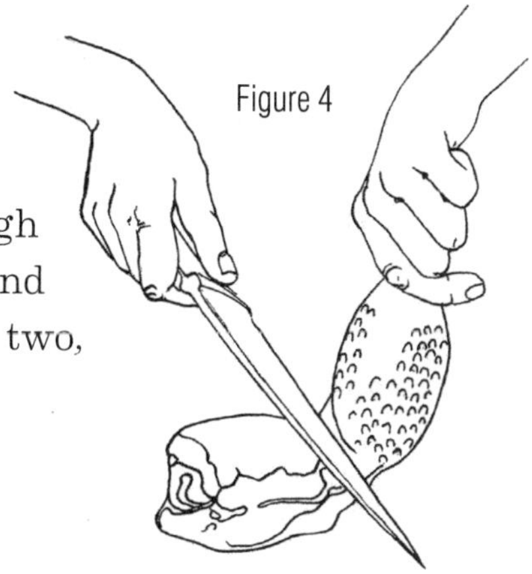

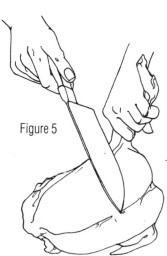

Figure 5

STEP 2: REMOVE THE WINGS

Lift the bird by a wing to locate the webbing at the joint. Slice through that webbing perpendicularly and circle around the joint, being careful not to take breast meat with it (Figure 5). Apply pressure at the joint and off comes the wing (Figure 6). Repeat with the other side.

Figure 6

STEP 3: REMOVE THE BREASTS

To remove the breasts, stand the carcass tail end up. Grab the breast side of
the bird firmly and slice down through the
rib cage to cut the back away from the bird (Figure 7). Lay the breasts bone side down and slice
through the middle of the two. Place the
heel of your hand on top of the blunt
edge of your knife and rap it hard
to chop through the breastbone
(place a kitchen towel on
top of the knife to cushion,
if necessary) (Figure 8). Now lay each
breast on the board, bone side down, and chop through
width-wise for four breast pieces (Figure 9).

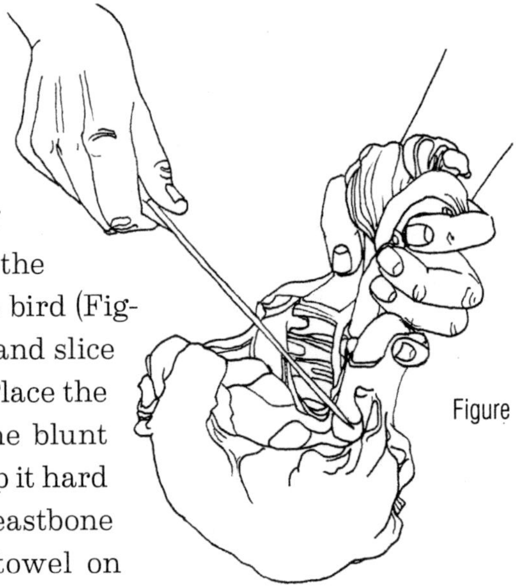

You now have the bird
broken down into ten pieces
(wings, legs, thighs, and
breast cut into two pieces
each), plus the back and neck for stock and the
giblets for another recipe—a lot of bang for
one bird (Figure 10).

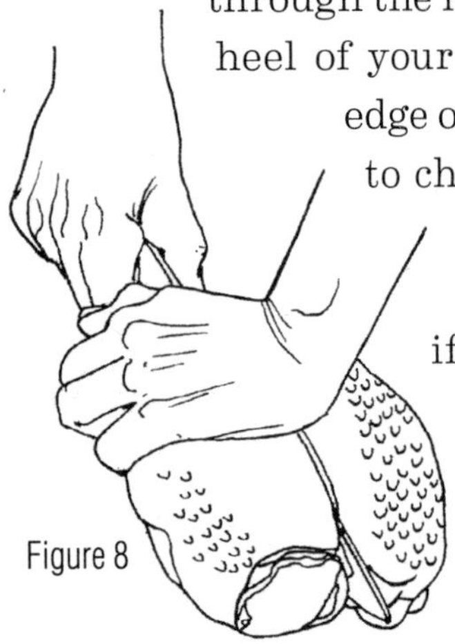

If you're not going to cook the chicken
right away, you can wrap it tightly and refrigerate it as you would the whole bird. Alternatively,
you can wrap the pieces tightly and freeze them
for up to three months.

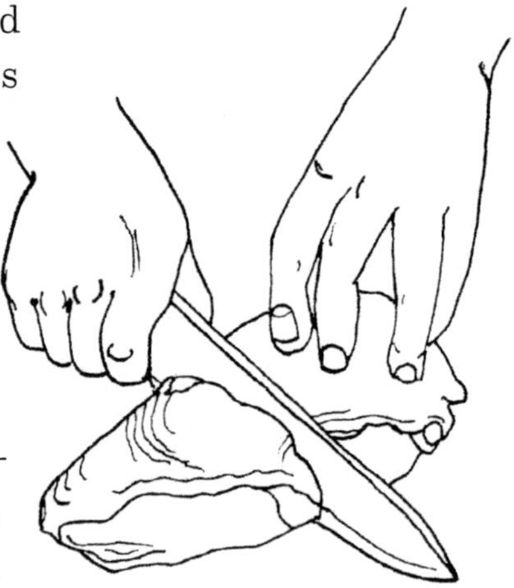

Figure 7

Figure 8

Figure 9

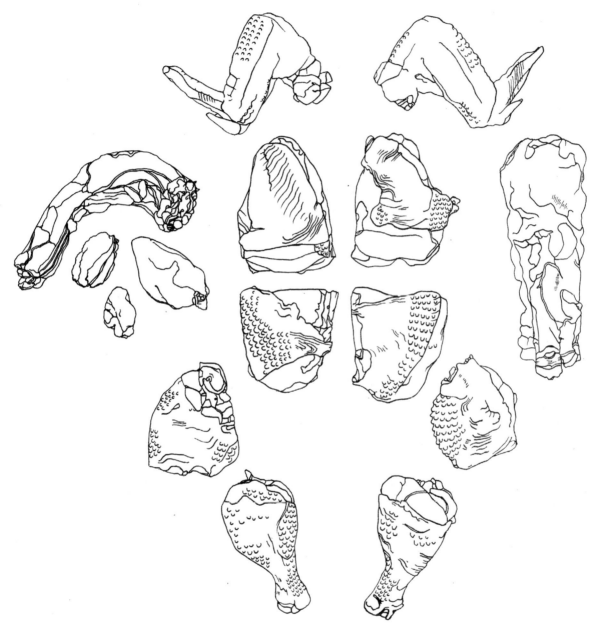

Figure 10

One Chicken, Three Meals

Here are three ideas that will help you get the most out of your good work—three meals out of one bird. It's a powerhouse strategy for weekday cooking. Each set includes a master dinner recipe, a leftover recipe, and soup idea. They are grouped together in trios that roll one dish into the next: Classic Flavors (Roast Chicken with Apples and Onions, Chicken Salad, and Chicken Soup, a.k.a. Penicillin in a Pot), Latin American Goodness (Arroz con Pollo, Burritos, and Posole) and Asian Combos (Chicken with Lemon Sauce, Chicken in Lettuce Wraps, and Congee). You can make the soup as your final step in each set, or save the carcass in the freezer and use it up another time.

CLASSIC FLAVORS

1. Roast Chicken with Apples and Onions
2. Chicken Salad
3. Chicken Soup (a.k.a. Penicillin in a Pot)

These three dishes feature time-tested favorites that will help you get multiple meals out of one bird without feeling like you are in a *Groundhog Day* version of meal repetition. Each one is deliciously distinct. The roast chicken is a terrific Sunday night meal that will fill your house with that "welcome home" aroma that, try as they might, cannot be bottled (or turned into a candle). Chicken salad will make your brown bagging a pleasure for beginning-of-the-week lunches. And a nice pot of chicken soup will be a welcome midweek comfort food if you simmer the stock overnight. If that's not in the plan for your midweek cooking, just freeze the carcass in an airtight bag and whip up the soup when you have some time to spare.

Roast Chicken with Apples and Onions

This is a comforting meal for a cool or rainy day. The apples and onions perfume the chicken and steam it from the inside out, so it's extra juicy. You don't have to make the gravy, but it's so easy, why not?

Makes 4 servings with leftovers

1 roasting chicken (5 to 6 pounds)

2 tablespoons unsalted butter, softened

Salt

1 apple, cut in half

1 onion, cut in half

1 shallot, minced

2 tablespoons all-purpose flour

1 cup dry white wine

2 cups Brown Chicken Stock (page 143)

➡ Preheat the oven to 375°F. Remove the giblet bag from the bird and reserve for another use (see page 120 for recipes). Pat the bird dry, inside and out. Rub the bird with the butter and season generously with salt. Stuff the cavity with the apple and onion. Place in a roasting rack set into a large roasting pan. Roast until the juices run clear and the internal temperature reaches 165°F when measured at the thickest part of the thigh, 1½ to 1¾ hours. Transfer the chicken to a cutting board to rest while you make the gravy.

➡ Set your roasting pan across two burners over medium heat. When the drippings begin to sizzle, add the shallot and sauté until translucent, 2 to 3 minutes. Add the flour and sauté with the shallot and the pan drippings until it just begins to color, about 3 minutes, to make a roux. Add the wine to deglaze the pan—dissolving and releasing the brown *fond* on the bottom of the pan. Use a whisk to scrape up the fond and blend the deglazing liquid into the flour. Pour in the stock, a little at a time at first, whisking all the while. Continue simmering and whisking for 2 to 3 minutes, to cook off any raw flour taste and thicken the gravy. Carve the chicken and pass the gravy separately. Leftover chicken keeps, cooled, covered, and refrigerated, for 3 to 5 days.

Chicken Salad

This salad bulks up a little bit of leftover chicken with some fresh fruit and vegetables, stretching the meat and lightening your lunch. This is a recipe for four servings, but you can halve or double the recipe, depending on the amount of chicken that you have. You can also make this dish with leftover turkey for a post-Thanksgiving meal.

Makes 4 servings

2 tablespoons mayonnaise

1 tablespoon strained or Greek yogurt

1 tablespoon fresh tarragon leaves, minced, or 1 teaspoon dried

1 scallion, thinly sliced

Salt and freshly ground black pepper

1 cup leftover chicken

1 apple, cored and diced

1 celery stalk, diced

1 tablespoon chopped walnuts (optional)

➡ In a medium-size bowl, combine the mayonnaise, yogurt, tarragon, scallion, and salt and pepper to taste. Add the chicken, apple, celery, and walnuts, if using, and stir to combine. Serve as a sandwich between toasted slices of whole wheat bread or on a bed of greens. The prepared salad keeps for 1 to 2 days when made with chicken that has been roasted no more than 3 days before.

Classic Chicken Soup, a.k.a. Penicillin in a Pot

Time-tested cure all or just a good dinner? You don't have to be under the weather to enjoy a good pot of chicken soup. I like to use rice in mine, instead of noodles, but once the base is cooked, you can add whatever you like. Herbs, such as tarragon or dill are a superb finish; add some hot sauce and lemon if that sounds right; or just leave it, as it is—a bowl of soul-warming goodness.

Makes about 2 quarts soup

1 chicken carcass

1 onion, diced

2 carrots, cut into coins

2 celery stalks, diced

½ teaspoon dried thyme

1 bay leaf

Salt and freshly ground black pepper

2 cups cooked rice or pasta

→ Place the carcass in a stockpot and cover with cold water by 2 inches (about 3 quarts). Bring to a simmer, lower the heat, and gently simmer for 2 hours. Strain into a heatproof bowl through a fine-mesh sieve, chinois, or colander lined with a double thickness of cheesecloth. Set aside for 15 to 20 minutes, to allow the fat to rise to the top of the stock. Remove any bits of chicken meat from the carcass and reserve. Discard the bones.

→ Wipe out your pot. Spoon 2 tablespoons of fat from the top of the chicken stock and add it to the pot. Skim the rest of the fat off the stock and reserve for another use (see page 113 for ideas for using up quality fat).

→ Sauté the onion, carrots, and celery in the fat over medium heat until translucent, 3 to 5 minutes. Add the stock, chicken meat, thyme, and bay leaf, and season with salt and pepper. Add the rice or noodles and simmer until heated through. Serve piping hot.

→ The soup keeps, without the addition of the cooked rice or pasta, covered and refrigerated for 2 to 3 days or frozen for up to 3 months. Bring to a boil and add the rice or pasta just before serving.

LATIN AMERICAN GOODNESS

1. Arroz con Pollo
2. Burritos
3. Posole

These three dishes all share a common flavor profile but are so different from one another. Arroz con pollo, chicken with rice, is a crowd-pleaser and a great meal for feeding a group, as it stretches the protein with flavored rice and vegetables. Burritos make the most of the leftover chicken and rice, complemented by "salsa bar" accompaniments. And a pot of posole—studded with hominy and garnished with fresh flavors—well, this special soup might be my favorite of all three.

Arroz con Pollo

I build this dish on a sauce, a sort of quick soffrito, which flavors everything in the pot. It's a combination of onions, peppers, garlic, and tomatoes that I blend into a puree. If you are going to make the companion recipe, the burritos, double the quantities of these ingredients and puree and reserve half of the sauce for the second recipe. Even if you aren't planning on the burritos for the next day, you might make twice as much of the sauce anyway and freeze it—it's a great base for lots of dishes. A dollop of the stuff will get any soup or stew off to a running start.

Makes 4 servings with leftovers

2 tablespoons neutral oil, such as organic canola

1 chicken, cut into 10 pieces (see page 144 for how to break down a chicken)

Salt

1 onion, diced

1 poblano or green bell pepper, seeded and diced

2 garlic cloves, minced

2 cups canned tomatoes with their juices (preferably home-canned), pureed

4 cups Blonde Chicken Stock (page 142)

➥ continues

ARROZ CON POLLO continued

1 teaspoon dried thyme

1 teaspoon dried oregano

1 bay leaf

Pinch of saffron (optional but recommended)

1½ cups uncooked long-grain rice

Freshly ground black pepper

Brown the Chicken

➡ Preheat a large sauté pan over medium-high heat until a drop of water dances across its surface. Add the oil and heat it until it shimmers. Generously salt the chicken and arrange the pieces in a single layer in the oiled pan, being careful not to crowd the pan. Sauté the chicken until it is well browned and releases easily from the pan, 10 to 12 minutes (if the chicken sticks, just leave it to sauté for another minute or two; it will release when it is ready). Use tongs to turn the pieces over and sauté until browned on the other side, about 10 more minutes. Remove the chicken from the pan and set aside.

Make the Sauce

➡ Add the onion and pepper to the pan and sauté until translucent, 3 to 5 minutes. Add the garlic and sauté until fragrant, about 2 minutes. Add the tomatoes, lower the heat to medium, and simmer until thickened, about 10 minutes. Puree, if you like (and if you have doubled your ingredients to make some extra sauce, puree and then divide the mixture).

Assemble the Dish

➡ Add the stock, thyme, oregano, bay leaf, and saffron, if using, and bring to a boil. Add the rice, another generous pinch of salt, and give it a stir. Return the chicken to the pan, season with black pepper, cover, and lower the heat to very low. Cook until the rice has absorbed the liquid and the chicken is cooked through, about 20 minutes. Remove from the heat and allow to rest, covered, for 5 minutes. Remove the lid, fluff the rice, and serve. Leftovers keep, cooled, covered, and refrigerated, for 3 to 5 days.

Burritos

Burritos are one of the best recipes for "upcycling" extra ingredients. Here, I'm using the leftover rice and chicken from the Arroz con Pollo (page 152). But with a tortilla, perhaps some lettuce, cheese, or avocado, any bit of cooked chicken, steak, roasted vegetables, fish, or beans can be turned into a tasty meal. If you've made a little extra sauce from the previous recipe, you can drizzle it in or grab any hot sauce you might have on hand to spice your burrito up a smidge.

Makes 4 burritos

4 large tortillas

1 cup cooked chicken, bones removed and warmed, preferably in the Arroz con Pollo sauce
(page 153)

1 cup leftover cooked rice, warmed

Arroz con Pollo sauce (page 153), or hot sauce

Fillings of your choice, such as shredded lettuce or cabbage, sliced cucumber, cooked beans, grated cheese, chopped tomato, sliced avocado, grilled peppers, salsa, guacamole, sour cream, chopped fresh cilantro, or scallions

➡ Toast your tortillas by laying them, one at a time, directly on the coils of an electric burner, over the flame of a gas burner, or in a dry pan over high heat. Use tongs to turn once.

➡ Lay a toasted tortilla in front of you (or line up all four, assembly line style). Add ¼ cup of chicken to the bottom third of the tortilla, keeping a 1-inch margin on the sides. Top with ¼ cup of rice, a drizzle of sauce, if using, and any fillings you wish. Be careful not to overfill your tortilla, or you won't be able to roll it. (Or pile on the fillings and eat it tostada style with a knife and fork.) If rolling, fold the bottom third of the tortilla over all the fillings, fold the sides over the filling and roll the burrito away from you. Place, seam side down, on a plate and slice in half. Repeat with the remaining tortillas.

Posole

Posole is a brightly flavored soup that is really filling and comforting. The recipe calls for hominy, maize kernels that have gone through a process called nixtamalization, an alkaline treatment that softens their tough outer hulls. Hominy has long been popular in the South but is widely available in the ethnic section of most grocery stores these days, in both dried and canned versions. You can find dried hominy kernels in the Mexican food section—they have great taste but require the extra steps of soaking and cooking. Canned hominy still has a pleasing texture and its ease of use might make it your new favorite pantry staple.

Makes about 2 quarts posole

1 chicken carcass (or bones from previous two recipes)

2 tablespoons neutral oil, such as organic canola

1 onion, diced

1 poblano or green bell pepper, seeded and diced

2 garlic cloves, minced

1 tablespoon ground cumin

1 teaspoon dried oregano

1 bay leaf

2 cups canned tomatoes with their juices (preferably home-canned), crushed by hand

1 ancho or chipotle chili, enclosed in a tea ball or tied in a square of cheese cloth

2 (15-ounce) cans hominy, or 4 cups cooked hominy, drained and rinsed

Accompaniments, such as crushed tortilla chips, diced avocado, sour cream, lime wedges,
    chopped fresh cilantro

➡ Place the chicken carcass in a stockpot and cover with cold water by 2 inches (about 3 quarts). Bring to a simmer, lower the heat, and gently simmer for 2 hours. Strain into a heatproof bowl through a fine-mesh sieve, chinois, or colander lined with a double thickness of cheesecloth. Set the stock aside for 15 to 20 minutes to allow the fat to rise to the top of the stock. Remove any bits of chicken meat from the carcass and reserve. Discard the bones.

➡ continues

POSOLE *continued*

➡ In a large Dutch oven, heat the oil until shimmering. Sauté the onion and pepper in oil until translucent, 3 to 5 minutes. Add the garlic and sauté for another minute, until fragrant. Add the cumin, oregano, and bay leaf and sauté for 30 seconds to release their oils. Add the tomatoes and simmer until thickened, about 10 minutes. Add the strained stock and chili. Simmer for 30 minutes. Add the hominy and any bits of chicken and simmer for 15 minutes to blend the flavors. Season to taste. Serve, passing the accompaniments separately. The soup keeps, cooled, covered, and refrigerated, for 3 to 5 days.

ASIAN COMBOS

1. Chicken with Lemon Sauce
2. Chicken in Lettuce Wraps
3. Congee

Why order carry-out when you can have great-tasting, easy Asian recipes at your fingertips? These dishes don't take a lot of time, they're super tasty, and will save your pocketbook—tip included.

Chicken with Lemon Sauce

This recipe has a combination of flavors that really works. The pan searing gives you wonderfully caramelized skin that's dark and full of rich flavors. The lemon perks it all up with its blast of citrus spike. The cornstarch thickens the sauce enough to cling to each bite but not so much that it tastes like gloppy take-out. Fresh and wonderful and from your kitchen!

Makes about 4 servings with leftovers

2 tablespoons neutral oil, such as organic canola

1 chicken cut into 10 pieces (see page 144 for how to break down a chicken)

Salt

2 cups Brown Chicken Stock (page 143)

2 tablespoons soy sauce

¼ cup freshly squeezed juice and zest of 1 lemon

1 tablespoon cornstarch

1 shallot, diced

2 scallions, thinly sliced

➡ Preheat the oven to 325°F. Heat a large sauté pan over medium-high heat until a drop of water dances across its surface. Add the oil and heat it until it shimmers. Generously salt the chicken and arrange the pieces in a single layer in the oiled pan, being careful not to crowd the pan. Sauté the chicken until it is well browned and releases easily from the pan, 10 to 12 minutes (if the chicken sticks, just leave it to sauté for another minute or two; it will release when it is ready). Use tongs to turn the pieces over. Transfer the pan to the oven and roast the chicken until cooked through, 25 to 30 minutes.

➡ *continues*

CHICKEN WITH LEMON SAUCE continued

➡ While the chicken cooks, make the sauce: In a medium-size bowl, whisk the stock, soy, lemon juice and zest, and cornstarch. Set aside.

➡ When the chicken is cooked, transfer it to a platter. Place the pan over medium heat. Add the shallot and scallions and sauté until the shallot is translucent, about 3 minutes. Add the sauce and bring to a simmer, using the whisk to scrape up any browned bits on the bottom of the pan. Continue to simmer until the sauce is thickened, about 3 minutes. Spoon the sauce over the chicken and serve. Leftovers keep, cooled, covered, and refrigerated, for 3 to 5 days.

Chicken in Lettuce Wraps

You can use the chicken from the previous recipe or any neutral or mildly flavored chicken recipe to make these wraps. If you are using the meat from Chicken with Lemon Sauce (page 157), you can add the leftover lemon sauce to the pan as well. Feel free to improvise further by adding any roasted or steamed vegetables you have on hand. Noodles or rice would also be a welcomed addition to this fun meal.

Makes about 12 wraps

1 cup Blonde Chicken Stock (page 142)

2 tablespoons soy sauce

2 teaspoons cornstarch

2 tablespoons neutral oil, such as organic canola

1 shallot, sliced

2 garlic cloves, minced

2 teaspoons grated fresh ginger

2 cups cooked chicken meat

2 cups cooked vegetables, noodles, or rice

1 teaspoon sesame oil

12 soft lettuce leaves from varieties such as Boston or Bibb

➡ *continues*

➡ Whisk together the stock, soy sauce, and cornstarch in a small bowl and set aside.

➡ In a large pan, sauté the shallot in the oil over medium heat until translucent, about 3 minutes. Add the garlic and ginger and sauté for another minute, until fragrant. Add the sauce and simmer until thickened, 2 to 3 minutes. Add the meat and vegetables and heat through, stirring occasionally. Transfer to a serving bowl and drizzle with the sesame oil. Serve with lettuce leaves for filling.

Congee

This traditional Chinese dish is commonly served for breakfast. But I like it as a warm, comforting dinner on a chilly night. The plain congee has a mild flavor—a terrific cure when you are under the weather. Consider it a base to build on. Add bits of meat or veg or a few shrimp, or keep it light with a poached egg or just a squeeze of lemon juice and a sprinkle of minced fresh cilantro.

Makes about 2 quarts congee

1 chicken carcass or the bones from the previous two recipes

1¼ cups uncooked brown rice

➡ In a large stockpot, bring the carcass and 3 quarts of water to a gentle simmer. Continue to simmer for at least 2 and up to 6 hours. Strain through a fine-mesh sieve. Remove any meat from the carcass and set aside. Discard the bones. Skim the fat off the stock and reserve for another use (see pages 113–119 for ideas for using up quality fat).

➡ Wipe out the pot and return the stock to it. You should have about 2 quarts. Add the brown rice, cover, and simmer until the rice bursts and thickens, or "flowers," as it's called, and the congee has the consistency of porridge, about 2 hours. Return the chicken to the congee, if you like, and add any seasonings or additional ingredients that you have on hand. Serve immediately or store, cooled, covered, and refrigerated, for 2 to 3 days. Congee will absorb liquid as it cools. Reheat over low heat, adding liquid to thin the congee to its original consistency.

Eggs

Too many eggs? That's easy to fix. Omelets, tortilla (the traditional Spanish egg and potato pie), and frittatas are all super and super-easy ways to put those extra *oeufs* to work. But what about half a dozen whites? Or extra yolks? Recipes that call for separated eggs can leave the home cooking hanging. The next time you face the dreaded "reserve for another use" clause in your recipe, you can either freeze your extra whites and yolks (see page 161 for tips) or turn to the recipes that follow.

The best-tasting eggs come from birds that are fed a natural diet and spend time in the fresh air and sunshine where they belong. You will see the difference in such eggs the minute you crack them open. The yolks are a deep saffron yellow color. Fresh well-raised eggs have tighter yolks that don't break as easily as older ones and maintain their shape in the pan. And good luck cracking them, too, as the shells of well-raised eggs are much sturdier.

When shopping for good eggs, you don't have to limit yourself to those from chickens. Duck eggs are rich tasting and a bit bigger than a chicken's egg. Quail eggs are tiny and perfect for hors d'oeuvres. Emu eggs, if you come across them, are gigantic and a deep blue-green color. One of them will make a frittata that feeds a crowd.

Prepping: The fresher your eggs, the easier they are to separate. Here's my favorite way to get the job done. Set out three small bowls: one for your yolks, the second for the whites, and a third as your "working bowl." Crack an egg on a flat surface and split it over the working bowl, allowing the white to drip out. Transfer the contents of the egg back and forth between the two shell halves until all the white drips into your working bowl and the "de-whited" yolk is all that remains in your shell half. Dump the yolk in bowl one, transfer the white to bowl two, and work on the next. Why the working bowl?

Because it is imperative that not a single speck of yolk taint your whites or they will be unusable in many of the recipes that call for them. By separating the eggs one at a time over the working bowl, you ensure that if a yolk accidentally breaks into the white, it will only affect the egg you are currently working on and won't ruin all the whites as it would if you were separating directly into the egg white bowl.

Storing: In other parts of the world, such as the UK, eggs are neither washed nor refrigerated—an odd site for an American visiting the supermarket there. Here in the US you can buy unrefrigerated eggs in farmers' markets in some parts of the country. They will keep this way for 7 to 10 days. Refrigeration will extend their shelf life. All eggs sold in supermarkets are washed, a process that removes a protective but invisible coating and reduces their shelf life. They are then coated with a thin layer of oil and refrigerated to extend the average shelf life of a supermarket egg to 3 to 5 weeks from date of purchase.

Freezing: Whites are easy to freeze. The best way is to freeze them individually in the compartments of an ice cube tray for easy measuring in the future. You can transfer them to an airtight container after they are solid. Defrost and proceed with your recipe.

Yolks are trickier. They need to be combined with sugar before freezing. Mix in ½ teaspoon with each ¼ cup of yolk and freeze in an airtight container. Suitable for baking recipes only.

WHITES

Oh, the egg white. So virtuous and pure. Their high water content makes them light and fluffy, particularly when whipped to high peaks by whisk or beater. You can take advantage of both of these outstanding features in the following recipes. Enjoy a light, powerhouse of a breakfast with the Egg White "Omelet." Or whip the whites up high to make crunchy meringues or fold them into sweet coconut for a gluten-free addition to the cookie tray, coconut macaroons.

Egg White "Omelet"

I call this an "omelet," in quotes, because, while it has all the elements of that classic breakfast staple, it deviates from the traditional technique for an easier, quicker path to curing morning hunger pangs. Rather than encasing the filling in an egg-based envelope, all the ingredients are cooked together.

Egg whites can be quite bland on their own, so give them a little flavor boost with fresh herbs and a hefty dose of vegetables to up the flavor ante. You can also add cheese, if you like. Here are a few suggested combinations:

Onion/zucchini/dill (feta, optional)

Scallion/bell pepper/cilantro (Cheddar, optional)

Shallot/mushroom/tarragon (Swiss, optional)

Red onion/tomato/basil (mozzarella, optional)

Makes 2 servings

6 large egg whites

Salt and freshly ground black pepper

2 teaspoons olive oil or unsalted butter

¼ cup onion, scallion, or shallot

½ cup vegetable of your choice

2 tablespoons fresh herbs

¼ cup shredded cheese (about 2 ounces)

➡ Heat a medium-size pan over medium heat until a drop of water dances across its surface. While the pan heats, whisk the egg whites until fluffy. Season with salt and pepper. Place the oil in the pan and swirl to coat the bottom. Add the onion, scallion, or shallot and sauté until soft and/or translucent; if using onion, 3 to 5 minutes, if using scallions or shallots, about 2 minutes. Add your choice of vegetable and sauté until tender. Add the herbs, stir, and add the seasoned egg whites. Drag your spatula across the bottom of the pan and rotate the pan to "spill" uncooked eggs into the ravine you've created. Repeat until the eggs are as firm as you like; it should take only 2 to 3 minutes. Remove from the heat and sprinkle with the cheese. Fold one last time to incorporate the cheese into the egg mixture and serve as is or perhaps folded into a biscuit, croissant, or toast for a hardy breakfast sandwich.

Meringues

Meringues are an essential technique for the home baker—and a no brainer to make if you have extra whites on hand. They make for the whimsical decorations on a büche de Noël, where their little puffs are transformed into the mushrooms on the Yule log. But they're tasty any time of year. Try baked meringues as the base of an elegant dessert, topped with berries and cream. Their crisp texture is hard to achieve on a rainy or humid day, so try to bake these when the air is crisp and clear—or you're well air-conditioned.

The key to fluffy, stable meringue is impeccably clean utensils. Use steel, copper, or glass—plastic can harbor traces of oil that will ruin your results. All beaters, bowls, and spoons must be absolutely clear of even a speck of oil. Any hint of grease and your whites will never climb to the heights you need. Wash everything thoroughly and then rub everything down with a little vinegar just to be sure. And be certain that not a whiff of yolk gets into the mixture—it, too, will keep the whipped whites from reaching their billowy best.

Makes about 3 dozen meringues

3 large egg whites, at room temperature (see page 160 for tips on separating eggs)

¼ teaspoon cream of tartar

¾ cup granulated sugar

½ teaspoon pure vanilla extract

Unsweetened cocoa powder, for dusting (optional)

➡ In a large bowl or the bowl of a stand mixer, combine the egg whites and cream of tartar. Whip until soft peaks form. Incorporate the sugar, 2 tablespoons at a time. Continue beating until stiff peaks form and the meringue is smooth and glossy. Add the vanilla and whip just to combine.

➡ Preheat the oven to 200°F. Line a cookie sheet with parchment paper or a silicone mat. Transfer the meringue to a piping bag fitted with a round tip or a large plastic bag with the corner cut off. Pipe 2-inch rounds onto the lined cookie sheet, leaving ½ inch of space between them. The meringues will each have a little peak shape. For rounded meringues, gently smooth the top with a moistened finger. Bake for 1½ to 2 hours, until crisp but before coloring. Remove from the oven and allow to cool for 15 minutes, then transfer to a wire rack to cool completely. Dust with cocoa powder, if using. Meringues keep for up to 5 days in an airtight container.

Coconut Macaroons

Coconut macaroons are one of those desserts that look so fussy but require minimal effort. Just three simple ingredients—egg whites, sugar, and sweetened coconut—and you have yourself a dinner party–worthy dessert. You can flavor them if you like. Almond extract is lovely; a little liqueur, such as Grand Marnier or Cointreau, is decadent. Dip them in chocolate and you can really up the "wow" factor.

Makes about 2 dozen macaroons

2 large egg whites

¼ cup granulated sugar

1 teaspoon pure vanilla or almond extract or flavored liqueur

2½ cups sweetened shredded coconut

➡ Preheat the oven to 325°F. Line two cookie sheets with parchment paper or silicone mats and set aside.

➡ In a large bowl, whisk the egg whites until frothy. Add the sugar and vanilla and whisk until combined. Add the coconut and stir until thoroughly combined. Drop tablespoons of the mixture onto the lined cookie sheets, leaving 1 inch of space between them. Bake until golden and crisp on the bottom and lightly browned on top, 20 to 25 minutes. Remove from the oven and allow to cool for 10 minutes, then transfer to a wire rack to cool completely. Can be stored in an airtight container for 3 days or wrapped tightly and frozen for up to 3 months. Defrost in their wrapping to avoid condensation from forming on the treats as they come to room temperature.

YOLKS

Electric-saffron-yellow-orange—that's the sign of a good egg. No matter what the label says, you can always tell a well-raised egg by the color of the yolk. Pale yolks come from a bland, pale diet of grain and nothing more. Deep, rich color comes from a deep, rich diet—the variety of grass, greens, bugs, and grubs, perhaps supplemented by a portion of grain, that is, the natural diet of a chicken—giving it and you optimal nutrition. When you've got golden yolks like that, it's a treasure you can't waste. Use them up in these recipes.

Mayonnaise

You can buy something called "mayonnaise" but until you make it from scratch, you have never tasted mayonnaise. I am not being a food snob—make some and I know you will agree. Homemade mayo has a creamy texture that is unmatched by anything you can get in the store. The ingredients are simple and shine when they are top-notch, so make sure to get your hands on some straight-from-the-farm eggs. The oil you use matters, too. Neutral oil, such as organic canola, will yield a mayonnaise with a classic taste; olive oil will render a spread that tastes of the fruit. Flavored mayonnaise—a touch of curry, tarragon, dill, or a spoonful of extra mustard whisked in—can serve as a dip or spread that raises the grade of everything it graces.

Makes about 1 cup mayonnaise

1 large egg yolk

Pinch of salt

1 teaspoon Dijon mustard

2 tablespoons freshly squeezed lemon juice

1 cup oil (see headnote)

➡ In a medium-size bowl, whisk the egg yolk until pale yellow. Add the salt and the mustard and whisk to combine. Whisk in the lemon juice. Add a few drops of the oil and whisk until it is fully incorporated. Continue adding the first ¼ cup of oil, a few drops at a time, whisking until it is fully emulsified before adding more. After that, you can add the oil very gradually, until it is fully incorporated. The mayonnaise will stiffen as the amount of oil increases, until you have a thick, spread. Keeps covered and refrigerated for 5 to 7 days.

★ **Note:** You can whisk in any of the following flavorings if you like:

Curry powder

Chili powder and ground cumin

Sriracha, Thai chili paste, or other hot sauce

Minced fresh herbs, such as tarragon, dill, chives, or cilantro

Lemon zest and freshly ground black pepper

Mustard and honey

Custard

Creamy, dreamy custard. English fruit crumble just wouldn't be a dessert without this luscious treat to top it. Try this recipe and you will never buy commercial pudding again. And talk about a use for extra egg yolks—this recipe uses up eight of them! It's not a difficult recipe to make, but you do need to temper the mixture—an easy technique of gradually raising the temperature of the eggs so that they don't scramble. Just follow along, keep the heat low, and don't boil the mixture and you will have a smooth, satiny custard that you can use to top desserts or serve all on its own.

Makes about 4 cups custard

3 cups whole milk

½ vanilla bean

8 large egg yolks

⅔ cup granulated sugar

¼ cup cornstarch

¼ teaspoon salt

1 tablespoon unsalted butter, softened

➡ Heat the milk and vanilla bean in a medium-size saucepan over low heat until hot but not boiling. Turn off the heat and allow to steep for 10 minutes.

➡ Meanwhile, in a medium-size bowl, whisk together egg yolks, sugar, cornstarch, and salt until well combined. Remove the vanilla bean from the milk. Slowly add half of the milk to the egg mixture, whisking vigorously and continuously until combined. Add this mixture to the remaining milk in the pan. Heat slowly over low to medium-low heat until the temperature reaches 170°F and the custard thickens, whisking all the while (the custard will thicken fully as it cools).

➡ Force through a fine-mesh sieve into a heatproof bowl. Whisk in the butter. Divide among ramekins, if desired, and press plastic wrap or waxed paper over the top of the custard, to keep a skin from forming. Allow to cool completely and serve, or cover and refrigerate for 3 to 5 days.

Hollandaise

My husband married me for my hollandaise. I have no doubt. It's not that my sauce is any better than any other. But more that I, certifiably "not a morning person," am willing to wake up on a weekend morning, bleary-eyed and rumpled, and make the stuff. Eggs Benedict generously napped with rivers of this luscious sauce—it's one way to this man's heart.

The bad news for us late wakers is that you can't make hollandaise ahead. The good news is that you can make it for dinner. Use it to top broiled fish or steamed vegetables, such as asparagus, for a meal worth marrying for.

Makes about 1 cup hollandaise

8 tablespoons (1 stick) unsalted butter

4 large egg yolks

Juice of 1 lemon (about 4 tablespoons)

Pinch of salt

- → In the top of a double boiler set over medium heat, gently melt the butter. While the butter melts, in a medium-size bowl, whisk the egg yolks until frothy. Add a tablespoon of water and whisk again. Add 2 tablespoons of the lemon juice and the salt and whisk to combine. Slowly pour the melted butter into the egg mixture, whisking constantly and vigorously. Add the egg mixture to the butter in the double boiler and whisk constantly until thickened. Taste the hollandaise and whisk in more lemon juice, if desired. If adding more lemon juice, return the sauce to the double boiler to thicken back up, whisking constantly. Use immediately.

Dairy

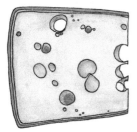

Milk is historically a seasonal food. Hard to think of it that way when you can pick up a carton or jug of whole, skim, 2%, or lactose-free at every grocery store, gas station, and big box store any day, any time of the year. But when animals are raised on their natural pasture-based diet, their milk reflects the abundance of their food supply—verdant, seasonal grasses.

The natural grass-based diet of ruminants, such as cows, maximizes the nutrition for the animal and the meat and milk they produce. Better for the beast, better for you, too.

The cyclical nature of raising animals on pasture is responsible for the creation of many of the dairy products we enjoy today. In times of peak production, it has always been imperative to preserve a portion of the milk so that dairy products could be enjoyed beyond the season. Yogurt, cheese, and butter are not only delicious, they serve a very important purpose—they are more stable and longer lasting than fluid milk, so they allow eaters to enjoy milk beyond its limited shelf life.

Milk preservation methods were particularly important before the age of pasteurization and refrigerated storage, when the shelf-life clock starting ticking the minute the milk left the udder. Modern methods of milk processing mean that we have a wider window of opportunity to enjoy a glass. However, many believe that when the milk is heated during the pasteurization process, particularly at the high heating levels required for ultrapasteurization, many of its vital enzymes are destroyed, reducing its nutritional benefit and making milk harder to digest.

I highly recommend sourcing milk from grass-fed animals when preparing these treats—the high-quality fat and nutrients it contains aren't just good for you, the results will be richer and more flavorful. Avoid ultrapasteurized milk in these recipes—it just doesn't perform as well.

MILK AND CREAM

You may not have thought of it as a technique that home cooks might have in their repertoire, but cheese making is a simple, fun way to use up excess milk. Making cheese, propagating yogurt, and churning your own butter will keep you from letting good milk go bad (cream, too!). They have a lovely lactic flavor that you can only get from being freshly made. And, bonus, they are some of the best examples of kitchen science at work. Watch as the pot of milk magically coagulates into cheese or as the cream transforms before your eyes into rich, creamy butter. Don't just save this alchemy for your eyes only; gather a crowd. Maybe sell tickets. The taste alone is worth the price of admission.

EAT IT UP! WHAT IS WHEY, ANYWAY?

Whey is the liquid part of the milk without the milk solids. Processes such as cheese making and butter churning separate these two components, leaving you with chunks of rich milk fat, in the form of butter and cheese curds, and the cloudy, liquid part of the milk, the whey. Many drink whey for its health properties. You can chill it and enjoy it as is or blend it into smoothies, add it to soups and stews, or use it to cook rice and other grains. You can refrigerate your whey for up to five days or freeze it for up to six months.

Queso Fresco

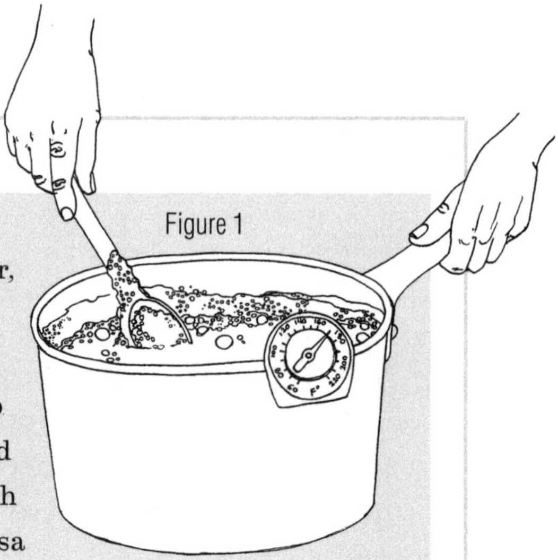

Queso fresco is a fresh cheese that is quick to make and meant to be enjoyed soon after, within a day or two. It has a creamy flavor, like a more intense version of the milk from which it is made. Queso fresco is also great in tacos or sprinkled over hot, roasted potatoes. It makes an easy app topped with a dollop of salsa or a drizzle of honey. You can season or flavor the cheese, if you like, by adding salt or other ingredients such as freshly ground black pepper, chili flakes, or fresh herbs, like dill, to change it up. You can also press the cheese overnight for a *fromage* firm enough to cook in dishes such as Indian saag paneer.

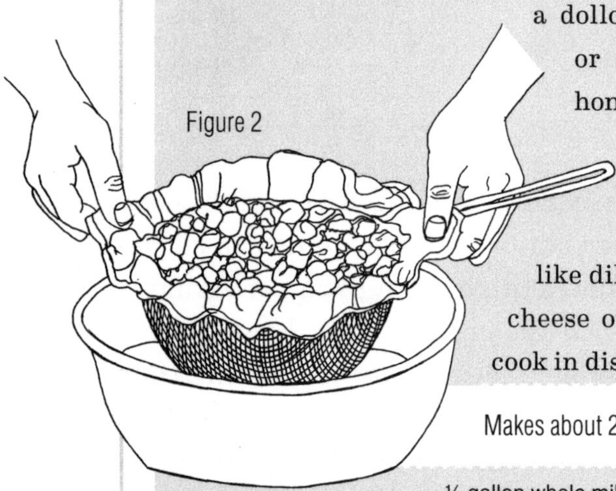

Figure 1

Figure 2

Makes about 2 cups queso fresco

½ gallon whole milk (preferably not ultrapasteurized)

¼ cup freshly squeezed lemon juice

Salt (optional)

Flavorings, such as freshly ground black pepper, chili flakes, or minced fresh herbs (optional)

Figure 3

➡ Heat the milk in a large saucepan over medium heat until it reaches 170°F, stirring occasionally to keep it from scalding. Remove from the heat and add the lemon juice. Stir gently to combine and allow to rest for 20 minutes, stirring occasionally, to allow the solid curds to form and separate from the liquid whey (see page 169 for whey uses) (Figure 1).

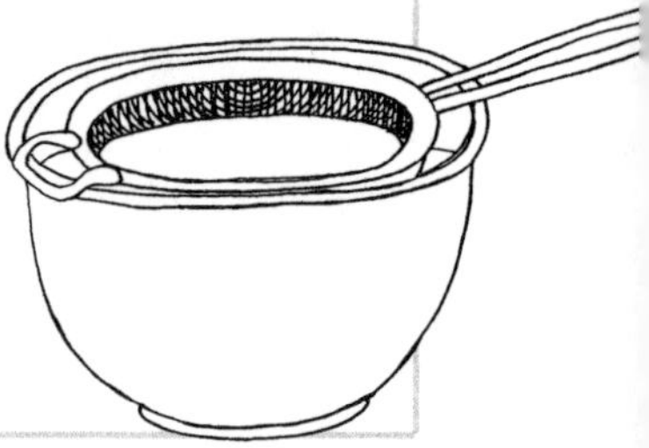

➡ *continues*

QUESO FRESCO *continued*

➡ Line a colander with a double layer of cheesecloth (arranged in an X, if necessary, to fully line the colander) and set it over a large bowl (one that holds at least 3 quarts). Strain the milk mixture through the colander (Figure 2). Gather the edges of the cheesecloth so that it forms a bag around the curds and lift it from the bowl to allow the majority of the whey to drain off (Figure 3). Lay the cloth full of drained curds on a plate or rimmed cookie sheet. Open the cheesecloth "bag" and sprinkle with a pinch or two of salt. Add any optional flavorings, such as herbs or spices, at this point. Use a spoon to gently incorporate the salt and any flavorings into the curds.

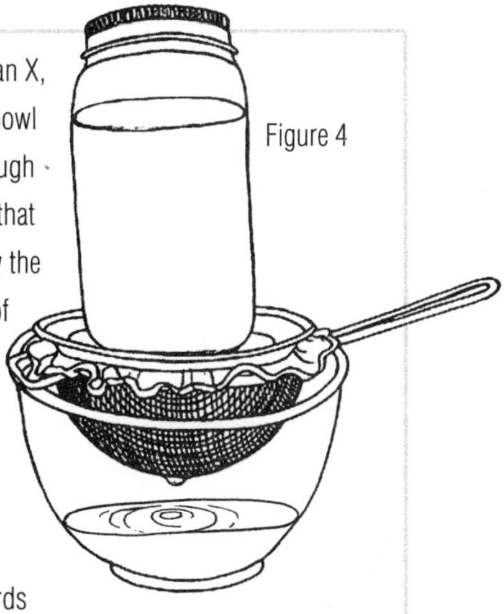

Figure 4

➡ Gather the cheesecloth up by the edges again to enclose the curds and twist it to squeeze out excess whey. Place the cheesecloth-covered cheese in a fine-mesh sieve and place over a medium-size bowl. Place a small plate on top of the cheese and top it with a weight, such as a can of beans or tomatoes or a canning jar filled with water (Figure 4). Place in the refrigerator for at least an hour and up to 12 to fully drain.

➡ Remove the weight, plate, and cheesecloth wrapping from the cheese and proceed with your recipe (Figure 5). After draining, the cheese keeps covered and refrigerated for up to 2 days.

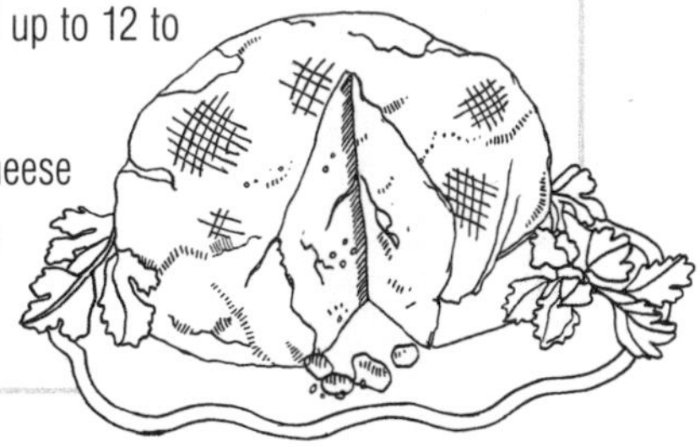

Figure 5

Crème Fraîche

Have extra cream? Make this luscious, not as tangy, cousin of sour cream. With a little less pucker power, crème fraîche more easily dances the line between savory and sweet dishes. Whisk it into recipes such as pureed soups where you would normally use cream. Sweeten some crème fraîche by whisking it with a little sugar and you can use it as you would whipped cream, to top a bowl of berries, or crown a slice of pie.

Makes about 2 cups crème fraîche

2 cups heavy cream

2 tablespoons buttermilk

➡ Combine the cream and buttermilk in a glass jar or small bowl. Cover with a tea towel or paper towel and set aside for 6 to 12 hours, until thickened. Give it a little whisk to blend it and it's ready for your recipe. Use it right away or cover and refrigerate for up to a week.

Butter

I love doing this little project with kids. It doesn't take long for the butter to come together and it is so dramatic—it gets a lot of oohs and aahs from the kids (and the grown-ups, too). Squeezing and rinsing the butter can get a little messy for wee hands, so be sure to have a few towels close by. And some nice bread for taste testing would be put to good use, too.

Makes about ½ cup butter

1 cup heavy cream

Salt (optional)

➡ continues

BUTTER *continued*

➡ Pour the cream into a jar with a lid and screw it on tightly. Shake the jar vigorously. After 2 to 3 minutes, small globules of butter will form. Keep shaking until a solid mass of butter forms in the jar, about 5 minutes. Scoop out the congealed butter, reserving the whey for another use (see page 169) and squeeze the butter to release any trapped whey. Continuing to squeeze it, rinse it under cold water to wash away any additional whey. (Whey left in the butter will reduce its shelf life.) After all the whey has been removed, you can massage in a pinch or two of salt, if you like. Cover and refrigerate for up to 1 week or wrap tightly and freeze for up to 3 months.

EAT IT UP! COMPOUND BUTTER

Compound butters, flavored with herbs, zest, or spices, are easy to make and bring an instant blast of flavor to any dish. Stir the following recommended add-ins into 1 cup of soft butter. Press into a ramekin or mold and refrigerate for up to a week or cover and freeze for up to 3 months. Stir into rice or pasta, or use to top just-cooked steak, chicken, fish, or vegetables.

Suggested add-ins: 1 tablespoon of minced shallot, citrus zest, or fresh herbs, such as chives, tarragon, cilantro, or dill; or ½ to 1 teaspoon of spices, such as chili or curry powder, freshly ground black pepper, smoked paprika, or any combination that appeals.

YOGURT

I always buy plain yogurt. Flavors are tempting, but limiting. Strawberry yogurt on your cereal? Delish! Strawberry yogurt in salad dressing? Probably not. Plain yogurt gives you maximum versatility. Blend it into marinades, dressings, and dips. And if you want sweetened, flavored yogurt, just whisk in a dollop of honey or jam and bingo, dessert time.

I also prefer full-fat yogurt for the luscious texture it provides without any unnecessary thickeners and binders. And if your yogurt is from milk from grass-fed animals, it has the "good fat," full of the same omega-3 fatty acids as wild salmon, walnuts, and flaxseeds.

Once you score the good stuff, you want to enjoy every last lick. Transform it into something truly fabulous, such as one of these tasty treats.

Tandoori Marinade

I make this marinade right in the yogurt container with an immersion blender. If you don't have one, you could use a whisk—just mince the garlic and ginger before adding them. There's very little prep, so it comes together really quickly. You can use it to marinate chicken or lamb, even dense meaty fish. The curry gives it great flavor and the acid in the yogurt tenderizes the meat. Magical stuff.

Makes nearly 1½ cups yogurt

1 cup full-fat plain yogurt

1 (1- to 2-inch) piece fresh ginger, peeled and sliced into coins (or minced if whisking)

2 garlic cloves, peeled (and minced, if whisking)

1 tablespoon curry powder

1 teaspoon ground cumin

1 teaspoon salt

2 teaspoons honey

Juice of 1 lemon (about ¼ cup)

Freshly ground black pepper

- ➡ Make the marinade right in the yogurt container: Add all the other ingredients to the yogurt and puree with an immersion blender or whisk to combine. The marinade can be used right away or covered and refrigerated for 3 to 5 days.
- ➡ To use the marinade, arrange up to 2 pounds of meat or fish in a shallow dish, such as a casserole, and toss with the marinade. Cover and refrigerate for 15 minutes to an hour for fish and at least 2 hours and up to 8 for chicken or lamb. Broil on HIGH 3 to 4 inches from the element until browned and cooked through (time varies, depending on the cut). Serve hot or at room temperature.

Fresh Herb Dressing

Yogurt makes this dressing creamy without being heavy. The fresh herbs add to the party bringing a lot of flavor, but in a light-handed way. You can use any tender herbs you have on hand, but I particularly like dill or cilantro in this recipe. Use the dressing for salads, as a dip, or drizzle it on roasted meat, fish, or vegetables for a lovely, light sauce.

Makes about 1½ cups dressing

1 cup plain yogurt, preferably full-fat

1 garlic clove, peeled (and minced, if whisking)

¼ cup fresh herbs, such as cilantro, dill, parsley, tarragon, or a combination (minced, if whisking)

Zest and 2 tablespoons juice of 1 lemon

½ cup neutral oil, such as organic canola

Salt and freshly ground black pepper

➡ Make the dressing right in the yogurt container. Add all the other ingredients to the last cup of yogurt in the carton and puree with an immersion blender or whisk to combine. Use immediately or cover and refrigerate for up to 5 days.

Homemade Yogurt

The best thing to do with the last bit of yogurt in the container? Well, make more yogurt, of course. The beneficial bacteria cultures in yogurt that give the creamy treat its flavor, texture, and belly-friendly properties are happy to propagate and do so prolifically under the right circumstances—which are very easy to achieve, indeed. Whole milk makes for thick, creamy yogurt.

The key to making yogurt is to nurture the bacteria so that it multiplies, thickening, flavoring, and preserving the milk. Think of it as bringing baby bacteria into the world and treat them as gently as you would a newborn, for the best results. You will need to keep the milk warm during the process, to allow the bacteria to flourish (between 110° and 115°F). You can do this in a number of ways by placing the bowl:

- In an oven with a pilot light
- On a heating pad
- In a cooler, surrounded by bags or jars of hot water
- Swaddled with a hot water bottle

Makes 4 cups yogurt

4 cups whole milk

At least 3 tablespoons plain yogurt

➡ To start, sterilize all your equipment (a bowl, tablespoon measure, candy thermometer, and a whisk) by submerging it in boiling water for 10 minutes. Keep the equipment submerged in the hot water until you need it. Bring the milk to a boil in a medium-size saucepan, stirring constantly to avoid scorching. Remove from the heat and allow it to cool to 115°F. Combine about 1 cup of the warm milk and the yogurt in the sterilized bowl and whisk gently to combine. Add the remaining warm milk. Cover the bowl and place it in the warm incubation area of your choice (see list of options). Leave it undisturbed for at least 5 hours and up to 8 (the longer the yogurt incubates, the thicker and tarter it will become). After the incubation period, chill the yogurt in the refrigerator for 2 to 3 hours and serve. The yogurt keeps, covered and refrigerated, for up to a week.

CHEESE

Cheese is probably my favorite thing to eat—breakfast, lunch, dinner . . . it's welcome at any meal (it's actually my preferred dessert). So, I usually have several different wheels and wedges in my fridge—all in different stages of blissful funkiness. When my selection dwindles and I am faced with a bit of this and that—some hunks that have even dried out a little or the odd rind or two, I turn to these tricks to revive and enjoy the last bites of cheese bliss.

Fromage Fort

This classic spread puts to use the rinds and drying ends from cheeses that are about to go past the point of no return—that bit of Cheddar that got forgotten in the back of the drawer, the bloomy rind that your flavor-fearing dinner guest left behind on the cheeseboard, a little wedge of blue that is starting to go more blue than you'd like. You can use any combination of cheese that you have on hand, just know that strongly flavored ones—such as those tasty blue cheeses—will dominate the flavor, but not in a bad way. It's traditional to use white wine here to moisten things up and make the spread more spreadable, but I prefer the subtle, nutty flavor of sherry (preferably dry sherry, lest we get too cloying). The spread benefits from a day or two in the fridge before serving, to allow the flavors to blend, but I can rarely wait that long. Scoop it onto crackers, dip into it with sturdy crudités, or slather the spread on slices of toasted baguette and run them under the broiler if you really want to send yourself swooning.

Makes about 2 cups spread

1 garlic clove

1 pound cheese rinds and ends, firm cheeses grated

1 tablespoon unsalted butter, softened, or heavy cream

½ cup white wine or sherry

Pinch of dried thyme (optional)

Salt and freshly ground black pepper

➡ continues

FROMAGE FORT *continued*

➡ In a food processor fitted with a chopping blade, drop in the garlic clove with the motor running to mince it. Add the cheese and butter and blend. Add the wine and the thyme, if using, and blend again. Season with salt and pepper to taste. Scrape into a ramekin and cover. Refrigerate at least overnight and for up to a week. Enjoy on toast or crackers. Top *fromage fort*–topped crostini with cooked vegetables, such as mushrooms, roasted root vegetables, or a few slices of olive, and run under the broiler for a quick hors d'oeuvre.

Mac and Cheese

Homemade macaroni and cheese might sound like a project, but you can make the cheese sauce—a classic béchamel with cheese blended in—in the time it takes to boil the pasta. Pop it in the oven while you make a salad or steam some vegetables and . . . dinner. The recipe makes quite a generous dish—our family of four usually has enough for at least another whole meal.

You can use any kind of cheese you want. Cheddar is common but I like to mix it up, often grating together whatever I have on hand. Nutty cheeses, such as aged Gouda, are great, but even something as assertive as blue cheese can be delicious and interesting as well. And if you have any extra tidbits on hand—some crisped bacon, steamed vegetables, a handful of cooked chicken—you can throw that in, too. Everything tastes super when it's covered in melty cheese sauce!

Makes 8 servings

6 tablespoons unsalted butter

Salt and freshly ground pepper

1 pound hollow pasta, such as rigatoni, elbows, or penne

1 quart whole milk

¼ cup all-purpose flour

12 to 16 ounces cheese, grated (less if the cheese is strong and assertive,
    such as very sharp Cheddar, blue, or washed rind cheeses; more if you have a mild cheese,
    such as Swiss), 1 cup reserved

½ whole nutmeg, freshly grated

➡ *continues*

MAC AND CHEESE *continued*

- ➡ Preheat the oven to 375°F.
- ➡ Butter a 9 by 13-inch casserole dish with 1 tablespoon of the butter.
- ➡ Bring a large pot of salted water to boil over high heat. When it comes to a boil, add the pasta and cook according to the package directions.
- ➡ While the water is coming to a boil and the pasta is cooking, make the béchamel sauce. In a medium-size saucepan, bring the milk to a gentle simmer over low heat, stirring occasionally to keep it from scorching. In a heavy-bottomed pan, such as a Dutch oven, melt the remaining 5 tablespoons of butter. Whisk in the flour and cook over medium heat for 1 to 2 minutes, to take away some of the raw flour taste but without coloring the roux. Add the warm milk to the pan 1 cup at a time, whisking vigorously after each addition until the milk is fully absorbed and the mixture is smooth. Gently simmer for 3 to 5 minutes to thicken. Remove from the heat and add the cheese, one handful at a time, whisking until fully incorporated into the béchamel before adding the next addition. Whisk the nutmeg into the sauce and season with salt and pepper to taste.
- ➡ Drain the pasta and add it to the pan of sauce. Stir well to combine the sauce and pasta. Transfer to the buttered casserole. Top with the reserved cup of cheese. Bake, on the center rack of the oven, until bubbly and browned, about 35 minutes. Allow to cool for 10 minutes before serving. Keeps, cooled, covered, and refrigerated, for 3 to 5 days.

Cheese Rind Soup

A cheese rind added to the pot brings amazing depth of flavor—not really "cheesy" but just a nice level of savory, umami flavor. I find the best to use is Parmigiano-Reggiano, but you can use any really firm rind that won't fall apart under the heat of the simmer.

This soup features the items we often have whiling away in the crisper. But you can try this little rind trick in any recipe—it's great in Italian wedding soup. Once you give it a go, you'll always keep a stash of rinds in your freezer just for the soup pot.

Makes 4 servings

2 tablespoons olive oil

1 onion, diced

2 celery stalks, diced

2 carrots, diced

Salt

2 to 3 garlic cloves, sliced

1 to 2 cups greens, such as Swiss chard, spinach, or kale (optional)

2 to 3 cups canned whole tomatoes (preferably home-canned), pureed

1 teaspoon fresh thyme

1 bay leaf

1 quart Blonde Chicken Stock (page 142) or Basic Vegetable Stock (page 107)

1 cheese rind, preferably Parmigiano-Reggiano

2 cups cooked pasta, rice, and/or cooked or canned beans (optional)

Freshly ground black pepper

➡ In a large saucepan, heat the olive oil over medium heat until hot but not smoking. Add the onion, celery, and carrot. Season with salt and sauté until softened, 5 to 7 minutes. Add the garlic and sauté until fragrant, about 1 minute. Add the greens, if using, and sauté until wilted, 2 to 3 minutes. Add the tomatoes, thyme, and bay leaf and simmer until thickened, about 10 minutes. Add the stock and rind and bring to a simmer. Lower the heat and simmer gently for 30 to 45 minutes. Add the pasta, rice, or beans, if using, and simmer until heated through. Season with pepper to taste and serve.

➡ The soup keeps, without the optional pasta or rice (but the beans are okay), cooled, covered, and refrigerated, for up to 5 days or frozen for up to 3 months. Bring to a simmer and add the pasta or rice before serving.

PANTRY

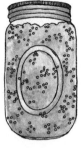

A well-stocked pantry can make it a breeze to throw together a quick meal. Items don't have to be expensive or "gourmet" to taste great. Local honey, some jam from a neighbor, a nice hunk of bread needn't come from a specialty catalog to be key elements in a terrific dish. On those occasions where you may be in possession of some little luxury that came in the holiday gift basket—yummy fancy olives, nice grainy mustard—these recipes will make sure that you get the most out of those treasures. And if, like me, you enjoy whipping up your own pantry staples— bread-and-butter pickles, strawberry jam—then you want to honor your good work by getting to the last lick of that jelly jar. Here are some great ways to do just that.

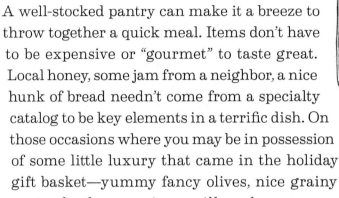

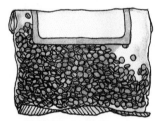

Bread

Fortunately, good-quality bread isn't nearly so difficult to come by these days. In addition to the artisanal bakeries that have become a part of many communities and farmers markets offering fresh-from-the-oven loaves, many grocery stores, too, have become a reliable source of just-baked bread.

If you're like me, the heel of a good loaf, particularly a baguette, rarely makes it home. That tempting treat is my reward for doing the marketing and I, like so many Parisians, break it off for a post-shopping snack.

Once I get my loaf, or what's left of it, back to my kitchen, I make a plan for it. Good bread is a living thing that doesn't take well to being shoved in the back of the larder and forgotten about. A little TLC is needed to make sure you get the most out of your loaf. Here's the plan:

Same day: If I plan on eating the bread that day, I set it on the counter, where it won't be forgotten. Sometimes I will cut off the other heel, or both if I haven't managed to munch through one in the car, wrap them up, and put them in the freezer for future bread crumb making.

Next day: If I am going to need the bread tomorrow, I will wrap it in foil to keep it from drying out and revive it by warming it in a 325°F oven before serving.

Someday: More than one day's wait, however, calls for a trip to the deep freeze. I wrap the bread in plastic wrap or paper and then again in foil, to keep out the cold air that can burn the loaf. When I am ready to enjoy it, I remove the plastic or paper, rewrap it in the foil, and then warm it in a medium oven, between 300° and 350°F (with or without defrosting), until it's heated through. Miss the boat on advanced planning? Bread that has gone a touch stale—or even more than a touch—can still be enjoyed. Try it in these recipes.

Croutons

Why buy croutons? Prepackaged croutons are full of unpronounceables and represent a serious upcharge. Make them at home, however, and you are turning stale bread into something delicious. Drizzle them with butter or olive oil, season with whatever herb or spice you choose and they taste so good, you will want to snack on them straight, salad or no.

Croutons made with a dense loaf can be tooth breakers. So, stick with a light, airy loaf, such as a French baguette, loaf of Italian bread, or even kaiser, Portuguese, hamburger, or hot dog rolls. These toast up with a great crunch but are delicate enough to add texture without dental work.

Makes 6 cups croutons; can be halved or doubled

8 cups (1-inch) bread cubes, from varieties such as those described above

2 tablespoons melted unsalted butter or olive oil

1 teaspoon dried herbs, such as thyme, oregano, marjoram, basil, or a combination

Salt and freshly ground black pepper

6 garlic cloves, unpeeled

➡ Preheat the oven to 300°F.

➡ Arrange the bread cubes on a rimmed cookie sheet. Drizzle with the melted butter, sprinkle with the herbs and salt and pepper to taste, and toss to combine. Smooth into a single layer. Scatter the garlic cloves among the cubes. Bake until the cubes are crisp and beginning to brown, 20 to 30 minutes, turning halfway through the baking time. Allow to cool completely before using. Croutons keep in an airtight container for up to 1 week.

EAT IT UP! BREAD CRUMBS

Save up your bread heels and any odd slices of stale bread in a bag in the freezer. When you've accumulated enough to merit washing your blender or food processor, make bread crumbs. Defrost. Tear into pieces and pulverize in your machine. Use as-is or toast in a dry skillet or 300°F oven until lightly browned. Crumbs can be frozen for 3 to 6 months.

Savory Bread Pudding

This dish is our favorite Christmas breakfast. You make it the night before, so the bread can soak up all the lovely custard. In the morning (or 8 hours later) pop it in the oven, let it turn brown and bubbly while you sit back and relax, then dig in. Delicious!

You don't have to save it for a special occasion, though; this dish is a winner for breakfast, lunch, or dinner. Master the basic recipe and you can customize it to your taste buds—and the contents of your fridge—at any given moment. It's that flexible. And that good.

Makes 6 to 8 servings

BASIC RECIPE

3 tablespoons unsalted butter

1 onion, diced

Salt and freshly ground black pepper

3 cups, total, any combination of add-ins (see below)

½ whole nutmeg, freshly grated

10 large eggs

1 heaping tablespoon Dijon mustard

3 cups whole milk

1 loaf stale bread (about 1 pound), cut into 1-inch cubes

8 ounces shredded cheese of your choice (such as Swiss or Cheddar)

ADD-IN SUGGESTIONS

Sautéed sausage

Crisp bacon

Crabmeat

Sautéed greens, such as spinach, kale, or chard

Sautéed mushrooms

Roasted peppers

Steamed asparagus

Steamed broccoli

■ continues

SAVORY BREAD PUDDING continued

→ Use 1 tablespoon of the butter to grease a 9 by 13-inch casserole dish and set aside. In a large sauté pan over medium heat, sauté the onion, seasoned with salt and pepper, in the remaining 2 tablespoons of butter until translucent, 5 to 7 minutes. Stir in add-ins of your choice and nutmeg to blend the flavors. Remove from the heat and set aside.

→ In a large bowl, whisk the eggs with the mustard until light yellow. Add the milk, 2 teaspoons of salt, and pepper to taste and whisk to blend.

→ Place one third of the bread cubes in the prepared casserole dish. Top with one third of the add-in mixture and one third of the cheese. Repeat twice more, finishing with the cheese on top. Press down lightly on the layers to compress them. Pour the egg mixture evenly over the top of the casserole. Cover with foil and refrigerate for at least 8 hours and up to 1 day.

→ Remove from the refrigerator and allow to rest at room temperature for at least 30 minutes and up to 1 hour. Preheat the oven to 350°F. Bake, uncovered, for 45 to 55 minutes. Allow to rest for 5 to 10 minutes before serving.

Stuffed Vegetables

Stuffed vegetables satisfy as a light lunch and make a super addition to a summer buffet. They look pretty on the plate—really showcasing the beauty of the produce. Lots of vegetables serve as good containers—bell peppers and even mild chilis, hollowed-out zucchini and squash, portobello mushrooms for mains, and smaller mushroom caps for apps. I put sausage in this stuffing, but you can leave it out if you want to go 100 percent veggie.

PS: This also makes a super Thanksgiving stuffing.

Makes about 12 cups stuffing

1 pound sausage (mild, spicy, chorizo, whatever you like), removed from its casing (optional)

2 tablespoons olive oil

1 onion, diced

2 celery stalks, diced

Salt and freshly ground black pepper

2 garlic cloves, minced

→ continues

STUFFED VEGETABLES *continued*

1 loaf stale bread (about 1 pound), cut into 1-inch cubes

½ cup pine nuts (also called pignoli)

2 ounces Parmigiano-Reggiano cheese, grated (about ½ cup)

1 teaspoon dried thyme, or 1 tablespoon fresh

1 egg

2 cups Blonde Chicken Stock (page 142) or Basic Vegetable Stock (page 107)

Vegetables for stuffing, such as peppers, chilies, mushrooms, zucchini, summer squash,

    or eggplant, seeds, ribs, and/or gills removed, hollowed if necessary (see sidebar)

➡ Sauté the sausage, if using, in a large sauté pan over medium heat until cooked through and browned. Use a slotted spoon to remove the browned sausage from the pan and set aside. Add the olive oil to the pan and sauté the onion and celery, seasoned with salt and pepper, until translucent, 3 to 5 minutes. Add the garlic and sauté until fragrant, about 1 minute. Remove from the heat and set aside to cool slightly.

➡ Preheat the oven to 350°F. In a large bowl, combine the bread cubes, sautéed vegetables, sausage, pine nuts, cheese, and thyme and stir to blend. Whisk the egg and stock together and pour over the stuffing mixture. Toss to blend and allow the bread to soak up the stock.

➡ Stuff the vegetables with rounded heaps of the mixture. Arrange on a cookie sheet and bake until the vegetables are tender and the stuffing is browned and cooked through, about 20 minutes for small mushrooms and up to an hour for large vegetables, such as peppers.

PREPPING STUFFING VEGETABLES

Prepare vegetables as follows (seeds, ribs, and gills can be composted, but feel free to dice any edible material and sauté it with the onions and celery in the recipe):

Bell peppers—Use a paring knife to slice off the shoulders of the pepper and whittle away the ribs and seeds.

Chilis—Slice in half, lengthwise, and remove the seeds and ribs.

Summer squash, zucchini, and eggplant—Use a spoon to scoop out the flesh, leaving a ⅓- to ½-inch shell

Mushrooms—Remove the stems and gills and hollow out with a spoon, if necessary, to create a bowl-shaped container

Panzanella

This is a splendid salad to serve in the summer; it has all the flavors of a good kitchen garden at the peak of harvest. It tastes quite light but the bread makes it a meal. If you want something even more substantial, you can add mozzarella balls, pearls, or cubes, some olives, diced chicken, or grilled shrimp.

Note: Soaking the onion in cold water removes excess sulfuric acid, which takes the edge off its bite and keeps it from developing a strong, sulfuric smell while the salad rests.

Makes 8 to 10 servings

1 load stale bread, cut into 1-inch cubes

½ cup plus 2 tablespoons olive oil

1 tablespoon Dijon mustard

2 tablespoons red wine vinegar

Salt and freshly ground black pepper

1 tablespoon capers

1 cucumber, peeled, seeded, and cut into 1-inch dice

2 large tomatoes, seeded and cut into 1-inch dice

1 green bell pepper, seeds and ribs removed, cut into 1-inch dice

1 yellow bell pepper (or another green pepper), seeds and ribs removed, cut into 1-inch dice

1 small red onion, thinly sliced, soaked in cold water for 5 minutes, and drained

1 handful of basil leaves, torn

Additional ingredients, such as olives, fresh mozzarella cut into cubes, diced grilled chicken,
    or grilled shrimp (optional)

➡ Preheat the oven to 350°F. Drizzle the bread cubes with 2 tablespoons of the olive oil and bake for 10 to 15 minutes, until beginning to brown. Remove from the oven and allow to cool completely.

➡ In a large bowl, whisk the mustard, vinegar, and a pinch of salt and pepper to combine. Slowly drizzle in the ½ cup of olive oil, whisking constantly to emulsify the dressing. Add the capers and stir to combine. Add the toasted bread cubes, cucumbers, tomatoes, peppers, and onion and toss to combine. Allow to rest for 30 minutes to allow the vegetables to weep a bit and the bread cubes to absorb the dressing and the vegetables' water. Add the basil and additional ingredients, if using, and toss to combine. Adjust the seasoning and serve.

Faux Parm

Those clever Italians, so crafty in the kitchen, so good at elevating even the most humble ingredient. Take bread crumbs, for example. The Italians turn them into *pangrattato*, toasted bread crumbs, seasoned with olive oil, garlic, sometimes a touch of anchovy, and a few red pepper flakes. They are a tasty alternative to Parmesan cheese when sprinkled on pasta and other cheese dusted dishes in its stead. Pangrattato adds great flavor and crunch. Here's my version.

Makes about 2 cups bread crumbs

3 slices or both heels of bread from a stale loaf

2 tablespoons olive oil

1 garlic clove, minced

1 anchovy, minced

Pinch of red pepper flakes

2 tablespoons finely minced fresh parsley

➡ Preheat the oven to 300°F. Pulverize the bread in your food processor or blender to make bread crumbs. Spread the crumbs thinly on a cookie sheet and bake until toasted and browned, about 10 minutes, shaking the pan once or twice to ensure even browning. Remove from the oven and allow to cool slightly.

➡ Heat the olive oil over medium-low heat. Add the garlic and gently sauté it, allowing it to infuse the oil without browning. Add the anchovy and sauté briefly, 2 to 3 minutes. Add the bread crumbs to the pan and stir to thoroughly combine. Add the red pepper flakes and parsley and stir again. Use immediately as a topping for risotto, buttered pasta, grilled fish, or sautéed or steamed vegetables.

Pain Perdu

You simply cannot have a section on using up stale bread without including the New Orleans classic, pain perdu. French for "lost bread," this recipe was developed to make something out of nothing—namely, stale bread that would be "lost" to the garbage bin if not for this recipe. It's such a wonderful example of clever kitchen trickery. Like so many recipes from the South, this recipe transforms a seemingly lowly ingredient into a downright sexy treat.

Makes 4 to 6 servings

8 large eggs

1 cup whole milk

1 cup heavy cream

1 teaspoon pure vanilla extract, or the seeds from ½ vanilla pod

⅓ whole nutmeg, freshly grated

Pinch of salt

1 stale baguette, cut into 2-inch slices

4 tablespoons unsalted butter

➡ Preheat the oven to 200°F.

➡ In a medium-size bowl, whisk the eggs until pale yellow. Add the milk, cream, vanilla, nutmeg, and salt and whisk to combine. Submerge six to eight slices of bread into the custard and allow them to rest for 1 to 2 minutes to soak up some of the custard.

➡ Meanwhile, heat a medium-size pan over medium heat. Add half of the butter. Using your fingers, fish the custard-soaked bread out of the bowl, one slice at a time, letting the excess drain off and back into the bowl. Add the soaked and drained slices to the pan and sauté until brown, 3 to 5 minutes. Use a spatula to flip the slices over and brown on the other side, another 3 minutes. Transfer to the oven and repeat with the remaining bread slices. Serve hot, topped with syrup or fresh fruit.

EAT IT UP! LEFTOVER COFFEE

I often have some coffee left in the maker at the end of our morning dosing. Sometimes it's less than a cup, but it can be much more if we've had to dash before our second cup. Either way, I hate to pitch it—particularly if I'm brewing up some of my special stash. When I have a cup or more, I pour it into a pitcher for an afternoon iced coffee jolt. Have just a few ounces? A good way to get the last bang out of your beans is to pour the last bits of java into an ice cube tray. Add them to cool coffee and they'll ice it without watering it down. Add the cubes to chocolate milk for an instant iced mocha. Pour that concoction into a blender and hit PUREE for an iced mocha frappe-la-la.

Pickles

When I was writing the "Put 'em Up!" trilogy on home food preservation, I got pretty tight with pickles. Developing recipes, testing recipes, tasting recipes, I was quite deep in the brine. As a sideline to coming up with new pickle recipes, I also came across some good uses for pickles and pickle by-products, such as their leftover brine. Whether you make your own or buy your pickles, these recipes will put your "extras" to work. My advice: for best results, use pickles with only ingredients you can pronounce.

Pickle Juice Fridge Pickles

You've finished the jar of pickles and are now left with a jar of brine. What to do? Make more pickles, of course. You can use this recipe to top up your brine and use it to regenerate a whole new batch of pickles. This trick is only good for one go round, though. The produce will dilute the brine too much for a second trip around the pickle barrel. And even if you did top up with straight vinegar, the flavors are too muddled to produce pickle perfection.

You don't need to stick to cucumbers here. Lots of vegetables make great pickles. Carrots, turnips, peppers, chilies, asparagus, green beans, cauliflower, onions, beets, radishes, garlic—yeah, you can pickle that.

Makes 1 pint pickles

½ to 1 cup pickle brine

½ cup distilled white or cider vinegar (5% acidity)

1 pound vegetables, as described above

➡ Pack a clean 1-pint canning jar with the vegetables of your choice. Place on a tea towel, to insulate the soon-to-be hot jar from the potential shock of the cool counter, and set aside. In a small saucepan, bring the brine and vinegar to a boil. Remove from the heat and pour over the vegetables. Allow to cool to room temperature. Cover tightly and refrigerate for at least 3 days and up to 3 weeks.

Pickle Backs

Ah, the Pickle Back. It's a little bit country; it's a little bit rock 'n' roll. The story goes that a southern gal turned a Brooklyn bartender onto the unexpected pairing of a shot of whiskey chased with a shot of pickle brine. The urban myth follows that drinking this dynamic duo allows one to see stars at night and suffer no ill effects the following morning. Might sound outlandish, but there is some culinary history to back it up. Russians often snack on pickles with their vodka for the same fun-with-no-fear reason.

Makes 1 drink

1 ounce not-your-best whiskey

1 ounce brine from the pickle jar (Any will do. Brine from bread-and-butters for the mild palate; that from a spicy pickle, if you dare.)

➡ Drink the whiskey. Drink the brine. Repeat as necessary.

Pickle Spice Mustard

My dear friend Luke Easter turned me onto this trick. Making mustard from the dregs of the pickle jar is an easy way to turn would-be trash into a zippy little spread. Of course, it helps if your brine is studded with mustard seeds, the common spice in many pickle recipes, such as bread-and-butter pickles and dills. You can mix the mustard half and half with mayo for an even creamier spread.

Makes ½ cup mustard

2 tablespoons pickling spice from the bottom of the pickle jar

2 tablespoons pickling brine

2 tablespoons olive oil

2 tablespoons mayonnaise (optional)

➡ In a small food processor or blender, puree the spices and brine to your desired smoothness. You may have to scrape down the sides a few times to ensure that the seeds hit the blades. Add the olive oil, a little at a time, and puree until incorporated. Add the mayonnaise, if using, and blend again, if desired. Cover and refrigerate for up to 3 weeks.

Pickled Eggs

Boiled eggs that are submerged in a vinegary brine are called pickled eggs. They are a refrigerator pickle—one that relies on the chill of the icebox to keep them safe to eat, rather than a processed pickle that is shelf stable. Although you may see jars of pickled eggs at room temperature—on deli counters and bars—you can be certain that these products contain additives and preservatives that inhibit bacterial growth. Homemade pickled eggs, made without added chemicals, are wholesome and delicious, and need to be kept well chilled at all times.

It's important to fully cook your eggs—no runny yolks here. So, observe the cooking time, even if it is longer than you would normally boil your eggs. The ice bath helps loosen the shells. You want to prevent splitting the whites, which will allow the brine to penetrate too deeply.

Some prefer the leftover brine from pickled beets, which adds a dash of sweetness and turns the eggs bright pink. You can use any brine from homemade or purchased pickles.

Makes 12 pickled eggs

12 large eggs

1 cup pickling brine, with bottom-of-the-jar spices

1 cup distilled white or cider vinegar (5% acidity)

➡ Gently place the eggs in a medium-size saucepan. Cover with cold water by 2 inches. Place over medium heat and bring to a boil. Lower the heat and simmer for 8 minutes. Transfer the eggs to a bowl of ice water and allow to cool completely. Carefully peel the eggs under a trickle of cold running water.

➡ Pack the eggs into a quart-size canning jar. Bring the brine and vinegar to a boil and pour over the eggs. Allow to cool for 30 minutes, making sure that all the eggs are submerged under the brine, weighting them with a small saucer if necessary. Cover and refrigerate for at least 2 weeks and up to 3 months.

Mustard

Mustard is an amazing ingredient. It can bring a tang and complexity to dishes without making them taste "mustardy." It plays well with all kinds of flavors—everything from citrus to sweet. It also has the magical ability to emulsify dressings so that they are smooth and creamy without any added dairy.

You can find a wide variety of mustards on the shelves these days. Hot to honey, there's a spread for you. While standard yellow has its place—my mom won't put anything else in her Maryland crab cakes—Dijon mustard is a pantry staple that I can't live without. It's the base for my house vinaigrette, makes a heck of a marinade, and will take your eggs—yes, your eggs—to the next level. Here are my three favorite tricks for putting mustard to work. Each of these recipes starts with a tip for getting that last little smidge out of the bottom of the jar—after all, with such magical stuff, you don't want to waste a bit.

Mustard Jar Vinaigrette

Not only does this recipe ensure that you use up every last spoonful of the mustard in the jar, it reduces dishwashing, something that is very important to me—and my dish-doing husband. All the ingredients can be combined right in the mustard jar, given a good shake, and the dressing is done. The jar is not only the prep bowl—it also serves as a handy, dandy dressing tote as well. Toss it in your bag, bento, or tiffin box for salad on the run.

Makes just over ½ cup vinaigrette

1 mustard jar with about a tablespoon of mustard on the bottom

2 tablespoons red wine or cider vinegar

Salt and freshly ground black pepper

½ cup olive oil or neutral oil, such as organic canola

- ➡ Add the vinegar and a pinch each of salt and pepper to the mustard in the jar. Screw on the lid tightly and shake vigorously to combine. Add 2 tablespoons of the oil, screw on the lid, and shake to emulsify. Add the remaining oil and shake vigorously until all is combined. (Alternatively, combine 1 tablespoon of mustard and the remaining ingredients in a medium-size bowl and whisk to combine.)

- ➡ Keeps, covered and refrigerated, for up to a week. Give it a little shake or stir before using.

Brunch-Worthy Eggs

Mustard in your eggs? You bet! The eggs don't taste of the tangy condiment, they just taste really good—savory and more "eggy." These eggs are great scrambled or as the base of an omelet that would be hardy enough for dinner. The zingy flavor also makes them a wonderful partner for any number of fillings. Mushrooms, spinach, any kind of cheese, bacon, sausage, herbs—all come to life when paired this way.

Makes 4 servings

¼ cup whole milk or heavy cream

About 1 tablespoon prepared mustard

8 large eggs (preferably from pasture-raised chickens)

Salt and freshly ground black pepper

1 tablespoon unsalted butter

1 cup of tasty bits, such as sautéed mushrooms or spinach, cheese, crisp bacon,
　 or sautéed sausage, or ¼ cup of fresh herbs (optional)

➡ If you are using up the last bit of mustard from the jar, add the milk to it and shake vigorously, then whisk the mustard mixture into the eggs in a medium-size bowl. If you are not trying to dislodge the end of the mustard, just whisk the milk, mustard, and eggs together in a bowl. Season with salt and pepper.

➡ Heat a medium-size skillet over medium heat until a drop of water dances across its surface. Remove from the heat and add the butter. Swirl the pan to coat the bottom with butter. Return the pan to the heat. Add the egg mixture and let the pan sit on the heat until the egg starts to thicken on the bottom of the pan, 1 to 2 minutes. Add the tasty bits, if using. Using a spatula, scrape two or three wide paths on the bottom of the pan, allowing the liquid egg to fill the gullies created. Repeat, forming large curds, until the eggs are cooked to your desired doneness. Divide among four plates and serve, perhaps with toast or roasted potatoes.

Mustard Glaze

Honey mustard–glazed ham is a classic "centerpiece" main that cooks have relied on to steal the show for many holiday celebrations. I've updated the glaze here with some herbs and spices that give it a fresh twist. You can use it to paint your holiday ham but it's also good for lacquering a pork loin or even a whole chicken or duck. It's best used to coat long-cooking cuts where the multiple bastings layer the glaze to shiny, amber perfection. (See sidebar for tips on basting.)

Makes 1¼ cups glaze

¼ cup apple cider

¼ cup prepared mustard

¼ cup cider vinegar

½ cup honey

1 teaspoon dried thyme

½ teaspoon ground allspice

1 teaspoon kosher salt

Freshly ground black pepper

➡ If retrieving the ends of the mustard jar, pour the cider into it, cap tightly, and shake vigorously. Combine the mustard mixture (or ¼ cup of mustard and ¼ cup of cider if you haven't mixed them in the jar) and remaining ingredients in a small saucepan and whisk to combine. Bring to a simmer over medium heat, stirring occasionally, until the flavors blend, about 15 minutes. Remove from the heat and allow to cool completely. Liberally brush your roast with this before and during cooking, every 15 minutes, until the last 15 minutes of roasting time.

➡ Keeps, covered and refrigerated, for about a week.

BASTING BASICS

When basting meat, it is important to follow a few kitchen safety rules.

- **Don't double dip.** A brush that touches a roast that is not full cooked runs the risk of harboring bacteria. To avoid contaminating unused glaze, portion out a basting's worth at a time into a small bowl and dip your brush into it, rather than the main batch. Refill the bowl as necessary, leaving the main batch of glaze untainted so you can store it, covered and refrigerated, for another use.
- **Don't baste late.** It's fine to use the same brush to apply glaze to the uncooked roast and to baste it throughout cooking. But be sure that your last daub is applied at least 15 minutes before you bring the roast out of the oven, to ensure that any bacteria lingering in the bristles are wiped out by the final blast of oven heat.
- **Don't lick the spoon.** The glaze is sweet and delicious. Avoid the temptation to swipe a finger across the basting brush or bowl of glaze that you are using to coat the roast. That's not a recipe for success.

Jam or Jelly

Making your own sweet preserves can be extremely rewarding. It's a great way to capture the flavor of locally grown fruits and, despite popular thinking, a pretty easy and fun project to take on. I love to make my own jams and jellies to have on hand and to give to friends throughout the year.

But jam making is not everyone's kink. If you prefer to buy your preserves, you can still use them in these recipes. Look for spreads that are made without high-fructose corn syrup, additives, or preservatives. All you need in a good jam is fruit, sugar, lemon juice or citric acid, and maybe a little pectin. The simpler, the better.

Jam Jar Martini

I came across the inspiration for this little treat at Matt's in the Market, at Pike Place, Seattle. Sadly, I was limited to water that day in preparation for a late afternoon book signing. But the first thing I did when I got home was to re-create this gorgeous idea, the "Breakfast Martini." Move over, mimosa, there's a new cocktail in town.

Makes 1 cocktail

2 ounces good-quality vodka

1 ounce freshly squeezed lemon juice

1 tablespoon jelly or jam, preferably homemade

Garnish, such as a lemon twist, fresh berry, mint leaf, or sprig of fresh thyme or rosemary (optional)

➡ Fill a cocktail shaker with ice. Add the vodka, juice, and jelly. Shake vigorously to chill and liquefy the jelly. Strain into a chilled martini glass. Garnish, if desired. Serve immediately. Recipe can be doubled.

★ **Note:** If you are using this recipe to rescue the last dregs of jam from the jar, add all the ingredients to the jam jar. Cap tightly and shake vigorously. Then transfer to an ice-filled cocktail shaker, shake to chill, strain, and serve.

Sweet-and-Sour Sauce

Maybe it's because I was a very picky eater as a kid that I am a big fan of allowing guests to tweak dishes to their liking. When I am feeding a crowd, or even my family, I like to offer a main dish that can be customized to the eaters' tastes. Having a variety of different sauces and unique condiments on the table lets everyone build flavor their own way. This sauce is a welcomed addition to the table. It's just right for grilled foods. It works so well with the smoky char. It's right at home with fried foods, too, where the citrus spike cuts the richness of the batter.

Makes about ¾ cup sauce

¼ cup apricot or peach jam

¼ cup freshly squeezed orange juice (about 1 orange)

¼ cup freshly squeezed lime juice (about 1 lime)

½ teaspoon chili paste or thick hot sauce such as Sriracha

1 teaspoon soy sauce

➡ If extricating the ends of the jelly jar, add the orange juice to it, cap tightly, and shake to dissolve the preserves. Combine the jam mixture and all the remaining ingredients in a small bowl and whisk to blend. (Alternatively, combine all the ingredients in a small bowl and whisk to blend thoroughly). Use as a dip for grilled or fried foods.

➡ Keeps covered and refrigerated for about a week.

Jelly Vinaigrette

Just a touch of sweet jelly elevates your basic vinaigrette. The pectin in the spread—the stuff that gives jelly its gel—is a brilliant emulsifier, binding all the ingredients in the dressing together into a velvety smooth texture. The sweetness cuts the bite of the vinegar—not so much that your salad tastes candied, but in a pleasing way, like when you swap out red wine vinegar for sweeter balsamic.

Even though the sweetness is an undernote, it is present and pairs with some things better than others. Probably not the best partner for fish. But try this vinaigrette in a salad of spinach, goat cheese, and strawberries; or peppery arugula, chicken, and blue cheese; mixed greens, grilled steak, and fingerling potatoes; or grilled vegetables, slices of pork loin, and fresh herbs. Jelly is the spread to reach for here. Jam, by definition, has chunks of fruit in it, which won't whisk together smoothly.

Makes just over 1 cup vinaigrette

1 tablespoon jelly, any flavor

¼ cup red wine vinegar

1 tablespoon Dijon mustard

Salt and freshly ground black pepper

¾ cup neutral oil, such as organic canola

➡ If using this recipe to clean out the jelly jar, add the vinegar to it, screw on the lid tightly, and shake to dissolve the spread. Transfer to a medium-size bowl and proceed with the recipe.

➡ Alternatively, combine the jelly and vinegar in a medium-size bowl and whisk to combine. Add the mustard and salt and pepper to taste and whisk to dissolve the salt. Slowly drizzle in the oil, whisking all the while, until emulsified.

➡ The dressing keeps covered and refrigerated for up to 1 week.

Jam Tea

Russian tea drinkers often add a spoonful of jam to their pot to sweeten and flavor their tea. It's best to start with a straightforward black tea so the flavor won't compete with the jam. You can add milk and sugar if you like, or drink it black, as the jam provides its own sweetness.

Makes 2 servings

2 teaspoons black tea or two tea bags of black tea

1 tablespoon jam or jelly, any flavor

Milk and sugar (optional)

➡ Bring a medium-size pot of water to a boil. Remove from the heat. Swirl a cup or so of the hot water in your teapot to warm it. Discard the water. Add the tea, encased in a tea ball, or the tea bags to the pot, followed by 2 cups of fresh hot water. Cover and let steep for 5 minutes. Remove the ball or bags. Add a dollop of jam to each of two mugs. Pour the steeped tea over the jam and serve, passing milk and sugar separately, if using.

Honey, Molasses, and Maple Syrup

Honey, molasses, and good maple syrup aren't just sweet; they are also full of character. Honey's myriad varieties reflect the flora of the fields traveled. From light, almost minty clover honey to dark, mysterious buckwheat honey, each has a flavor that speaks distinctly of the bees' seasonal diet. Molasses, the by-product of refining white sugar, has all the rich complexity of long-boiled sugarcane, just like its cousin, a fine, well-aged rum. Maple syrup, tapped when days are warm but nights still turn chilly, has a rich, deep flavor reminiscent of cozy winter breakfasts.

When shopping for these three sweet things, you want to make sure you get the real thing, not artificial flavorings. The best place to shop for them is directly from the source, if you can—honey is a staple at most farmers' markets and maple syrup at those in the Northeast. My mother brings me my molasses from a hardware store in South Carolina, where they dispense it from a large vat by the jelly jar. Lucky me! But if you can't get your honey, molasses, or syrup from the source, read the label. Each should contain one ingredient only.

Honey, molasses, and maple syrup all come in various grades, from light to dark. I prefer the darkest of all three for better flavor and more. Dark honeys, such as buckwheat and chestnut, taste smoky and nuanced. Blackstrap molasses, from the last boiling of the sugarcane refining process, has not only layers of flavor but is loaded with minerals. And when it comes to maple syrup, I always reach for Grade B. While it is reserved by many strictly for use in recipes, I prefer its deep maple character to the lighter, more refined Grade A on my pancakes. I encourage you to seek out the funkier versions of these ingredients, but any type will work in these recipes.

Citrus-Glazed Carrots

"Glazed carrots" can sound kind of retro in a 1950s casserole kind of way, but when you cook them in this citrus-spiked braise, they're anything but dated. I like the maple flavor here, but you could use honey, too. Dark honey, such as buckwheat, gives the veg the same burnt sugar edge that the syrup offers.

Makes 4 servings

Zest and juice of 1 orange (about ½ cup)

2 tablespoons pure maple syrup or dark honey

2 tablespoons unsalted butter

1 pound carrots, peeled and halved width-wise

Salt and freshly ground black pepper

➡ If you are using this recipe to enjoy the last licks of honey or syrup in the jar or jug, swirl the citrus juice in the container and then proceed with the recipe. Otherwise, combine the orange zest and juice and syrup in a small bowl and whisk to combine. Heat a medium-size sauté pan over medium heat. Add the butter, carrots, and a pinch each of salt and pepper to taste and sauté until lightly browned in spots, 3 to 5 minutes. Add the juice mixture, lower the heat, partially cover, and simmer until nearly tender, about 5 minutes (you can add a splash of water if the carrots need a few more minutes to cook through). Uncover and sauté until the glaze thickens and coats the carrots. Adjust the seasoning and serve.

Teriyaki Salmon

Molasses has a complex minerality that sets it apart from other sweeteners. This depth of flavor has a sort of hardiness all its own—the bass note to refined sugar's treble—so it plays beautifully with savory foods. The combination of sweet yet earthy molasses, fiery ginger, and the sting of the vinegar hits your taste buds in all the right places.

Makes 4 to 6 servings

2 tablespoons blackstrap molasses

¼ cup rice vinegar

¼ cup soy sauce

2 tablespoons neutral oil, such as organic canola, plus more for broiler rack

1 (2-inch) knob fresh ginger, peeled and sliced into coins

2 garlic cloves, peeled

1 (2-pound) piece wild salmon

➡ If you are using this recipe to get at the last of the molasses, add the vinegar to the jar, screw on the lid, and shake vigorously. Then proceed with the recipe.

➡ Otherwise, puree the molasses, vinegar, soy sauce, oil, ginger, and garlic in a blender or the cup of an immersion blender. Place the salmon in a bowl or casserole large enough for it to lie flat and pour the sauce over it. Cover and refrigerate for at least 15 minutes and up to 1 hour.

➡ Preheat the broiler. Lightly coat a broiler rack or cake cooling rack with oil (if using a cake cooling rack, place it on an aluminum-covered cookie sheet). Remove the fish from the marinade and let the excess drip off. Place the fish, skin side up, on the rack. Broil, 3 inches from the element, until the skin is well charred, about 5 minutes.

➡ While the fish is cooking, transfer the marinade to a small saucepan, add ½ cup of water, and boil for 10 minutes, until reduced by half.

➡ Using a fish spatula or two regular spatulas, turn the fish over. Remove the fish from the broiler, pour a few tablespoons of the marinade onto the fish, and return the fish to the broiler. Broil the fish until it is beginning to char and is nearly opaque in the middle. Allow to rest 5 minutes before serving. Cut the fish into portions and serve, passing the sauce separately.

Pomegranate Chicken

Fesenjan is a sexy-delicious Middle Eastern dish of slow-simmered chicken, walnuts, and pomegranate. I became a fan years ago at one of the most romantic little restaurants—an Afghani restaurant just a few blocks from my apartment in the East Village of New York. My then sweetheart, now husband, and I spent a most memorable meal there one winter's night. Giant, feather-size snowflakes falling down, the two of us cross-legged on pillows around a low, window-side table, and this dish. Make it for your next at-home date night.

Makes 4 to 6 servings

2 tablespoons molasses

2 cups pomegranate juice

2 tablespoons neutral oil, such as organic canola

2 pounds boneless, skinless chicken thighs, cut into thirds

1 onion, diced

Salt and freshly ground black pepper

1 cinnamon stick

1 bay leaf

1 teaspoon cornstarch

½ cup walnuts, chopped

➡ If you want to get the last of the molasses out of the jar, add ½ cup of the pomegranate juice, screw on the lid tightly, and shake. Then proceed with the recipe. Otherwise, start by cooking the chicken.

➡ Heat a large sauté pan over medium heat. Pour in the oil and swirl to coat the pan. Add the chicken and sauté, stirring occasionally, until lightly browned. Add the onion, season with salt and pepper, and sauté until the onion becomes translucent, 3 to 5 minutes. Add 1½ cups of the pomegranate juice, the molasses (or the jar mixture plus an additional cup of juice), and the cinnamon stick and bay leaf, partially cover, and bring to a simmer. Continue to simmer until the chicken is very tender, about 30 minutes.

➡ Use a spatula or wooden spoon to roughly break the tender chicken into bite-size pieces. Combine the remaining ½ cup of juice and the cornstarch in a small bowl. Add the cornstarch mixture to the pan, whisking to combine. Add the walnuts. Simmer, uncovered, for an additional 10 to 15 minutes, until the sauce is thickened and the walnuts are tender. Serve over rice or couscous.

Blue Cheese Crostini with Sherry Drizzle

I just adore cheese as dessert. With a digestif? Even better. Preferably something sweet, but not cloying, such as a nice medium-dry sherry. That was the inspiration for this dish—that classic flavor combination, but as a cocktail nibble, rather than an after-dinner treat. You can make the drizzle and toast the crostini ahead of time. Then just assemble the snack right before you serve it. It's as simple as your standard cheese and crackers, but much more inviting.

Note: The alcohol in this recipe makes it "adults only."

Makes about 24 crostini

1 French baguette, cut into 24 slices

1 tablespoon good-quality olive oil

2 tablespoons honey, preferably a dark variety

1 tablespoon dry sherry

Freshly ground black pepper

¼ pound good-quality blue cheese, preferably domestic, such as Bayley Hazen Blue on the East
   Coast or Point Reyes Original Blue on the West Coast

➡ Preheat the broiler. Arrange the baguette slices on a cookie sheet and drizzle with the olive oil. Broil, 3 inches from the element, until browned, 1 to 2 minutes. Turn the slices over and broil the other side until browned, another 1 to 2 minutes. Remove from the broiler and allow to cool completely. Once completely cooled, the crostini can be stored, covered, for up to 2 days. Refresh by heating in a 350°F oven for 5 minutes and allow to cool to room temperature.

➡ If using this recipe to get the last bit of honey out of the jar, place the jar in a pan of gently simmering water to thin it. Add the sherry and pepper, twist on the lid, and shake vigorously. Otherwise, combine the honey, sherry, and a pinch of pepper in a small bowl and whisk until blended.

➡ Arrange the crostini on a serving platter. Top with crumbles of the blue cheese. Drizzle with the honey mixture and serve.

Pureed Squash Soup

A little maple syrup in this soup is just enough to point up the sweetness of the veg without making it taste like candy. Cinnamon and cloves add to the warmth of the dish. I like to garnish the soup with something that contrasts with its smooth texture and fireside flavors. The crunch of nuts or croutons and a swirl of sour cream or yogurt would all be welcome here.

Makes 4 servings

2 tablespoons pure maple syrup

1 quart Blonde Chicken Stock (page 142) or water

1 butternut squash

1 tablespoon olive oil

Salt and freshly ground black pepper

2 tablespoons unsalted butter

1 onion, diced

1 garlic clove, minced

½ teaspoon ground cinnamon

¼ teaspoon ground cloves

Garnishes, such as toasted walnuts or hull-less pumpkin seeds (pepitas) (page 89), croutons, sour cream, yogurt, walnut oil, or Parsley Oil (page 82)

➡ If you are trying to extricate the last of the syrup from the jug, add ½ cup of the stock or water to it, screw on the lid and shake like mad. Proceed with the recipe. Otherwise, start by roasting the squash.

➡ Preheat the oven to 375°F.

➡ Cut the squash in half, lengthwise. Cut off the round ends of the squash and remove the seeds. Cut the straight part of the squash in half, lengthwise, again. Place the pieces in a large casserole dish, rub them all over with the olive oil, season with salt and pepper, and roast until tender, about 30 minutes. When cool enough to handle, remove the skin and roughly chop the flesh.

➡ *continues*

PUREED SQUASH SOUP *continued*

→ In a medium-size saucepan, sauté the onion, seasoned with salt and pepper, in the butter over medium heat until translucent, 3 to 5 minutes. Add the garlic and sauté until fragrant, about 1 minute. Add the cinnamon and cloves and stir to refresh the spices. Add the syrup, stock (or the jar mixture plus the remaining stock), and squash and simmer to combine the flavors, 15 to 20 minutes. Puree with an immersion blender or in a standard blender, working in batches if necessary. Divide among four bowls and garnish as you like.

→ Keeps, cooled, covered, and refrigerated, for up to 3 days, and frozen for up to 3 months. Bring to a simmer and garnish just before serving.

Olive Juice

"Olive juice, olive juice, olive juice." Mouthed across a crowded room, it can look like a declaration of love (actors sometimes substitute it for those three little words) . . . or just a cry for a dirty martini. You may not think of olive juice as a thing of value, but it can be a tasty ingredient if you know what to do with it. That briny, slightly oily liquid in the bottom of your olive jar is full of great flavor and can be used in a number of ways. You can use the juice from any variety of olive, but avoid those that contain a lot of preservatives. Olives that are bottled with vinegar, water, and salt will stay fresh in the fridge just fine, so no need to load up on the chemistry.

Dirty Martini

Dirty Martinis are my favorite martinis. Really dirty—I like mine loaded with enough brine to taste like the sea. Salty and bracing with extra olives in the glass—it's a drink and a snack all in one.

Makes 1 cocktail

2 ounces very good vodka

½ to 1 ounce olive juice

½ ounce dry vermouth

3 olives, for garnish

➡ Combine the vodka, olive juice, and vermouth in a cocktail shaker full of ice. Cover and shake until thoroughly chilled, about 1 minute. Strain into a chilled martini glass and garnish with three olives speared on a toothpick.

Olive Vinaigrette

The briny olive juice gives this vinaigrette a head start in the taste department. Use it to supplement the vinegar in your recipe for a little olive-y punch. Great on salads, sure, but try it as marinade for chicken or mild cheese, such as mozzarella balls or cubes—it's out of this world.

Makes just under 1 cup vinaigrette

¼ cup olive juice

2 tablespoons red wine vinegar

Freshly ground black pepper

½ cup olive oil

➡ In a small bowl, whisk together the olive juice, vinegar, and pepper. Slowly whisk in the olive oil, a little at a time. Keeps, covered and refrigerated, for up to 5 days.

Tapenade

This olive spread is a French kitchen staple. It's a handy little recipe to have up your sleeve when company pops by, the kids are screaming for a snack, or you're just plum out of ideas for lunch. Serve it on toasted baguette slices, maybe with some goat cheese or feta, or toss it with cooled pasta and tomatoes, perhaps with some diced leftover chicken, for the easiest pasta salad.

Makes ¾ cup tapenade

¼ cup olive juice

½ cup olives

2 anchovy fillets (optional)

1 garlic clove

¼ cup fresh flat-leaf parsley leaves (see pages 81–83 for using up parsley stems)

➡ In a standard blender or using an immersion blender, puree all the ingredients until smooth. Use immediately or refrigerate, covered, for up to 5 days.

5 A LITTLE EXTRA— UPCYCLING

Leftovers don't need to be a retread of last night's meal, run through the microwave and tasting like a lesser version of their original selves. Oh no, think of leftovers as secret ingredients—a running start on a totally fresh, totally delicious new meal. Having a cup or two of cooked and ready meat, veg, and pasta and/or rice will shave ages off meal prep. By "upcycling" these ingredients, you'll save time, energy, and money by stretching a little bit of this and that into a feast and you'll have a tasty, homemade meal at your fingertips any day of the week. The following recipes will show you how.

Croquettes

Extra mashed potatoes take on an elegant persona in this classic appetizer. You need to start with cooled, mashed potatoes anyway, so it's a perfect way to eat up your extra spuds. Frankly, I find starting the recipe from zero—with fresh potatoes that have to be peeled, boiled, mashed, and cooled—too much of a bother. But if you're ahead of the game, with the cooled mash already on hand, well, then, this dish is a snap. It's a joy to serve as a nibble during cocktail hour or as a passed snack on game day.

Makes about 12 croquettes

2 cups cooked, cooled mashed potatoes

¼ cup all-purpose flour

3 large eggs

¼ cup grated cheese, such as Parmigiano-Reggiano, Swiss, or Cheddar

2 tablespoons finely minced ham or crumbled bacon (optional)

Salt and freshly ground black pepper

2 cups fine bread crumbs (see page 184)

1 cup neutral oil, such as organic canola

Dijon mayo (¼ cup mayonnaise, 2 tablespoons Dijon mustard, whisked to combine)

➡ Combine the potatoes, flour, one of the eggs, the cheese, bacon, if using, and salt and pepper and stir with a fork until thoroughly blended. Using damp hands, form into logs about 2 inches long and 1 inch in diameter, placing them on a parchment-covered cookie sheet as you go. When all the logs are formed, refrigerate for 30 minutes.

➡ Beat the remaining 2 eggs in a small, shallow bowl and set aside. Place the crumbs in another shallow bowl. Dip a potato log into the beaten egg, then into the bread crumbs, shaking off any excess. Return them to the cookie sheet. Refrigerate the coated logs for an additional 30 minutes.

➡ Heat the oil in a medium-size sauté pan over medium heat until shimmering. Add the logs, working in batches if necessary to avoid crowding. Fry until browned, about 3 minutes per side. Serve hot with the Dijon mayo for dipping.

Empanadas

My husband was born in Argentina, and when I made my inaugural pilgrimage to his city of birth, I believe I ate my weight in empanadas, one of the signature dishes of the country. These light pastry pockets are stuffed with all manner of fillings from sweet to savory—ground beef, olive, and raisin being the most traditional. But you don't have to stop there. Empanadas are the original "hot pocket" and you can use whatever you have available to make a tasty handheld meal. Follow this master recipe and try some of the suggested combinations or come up with some of your own. Make extra and freeze—they reheat beautifully in a 325°F oven.

Note: Chilled ingredients result in the flakiest dough, so cool everything as directed and work swiftly.

Makes about 12 empanadas

DOUGH

2¼ cups all-purpose flour, frozen for 30 minutes, plus more for dusting

1½ teaspoons salt

8 tablespoons (1 stick) unsalted butter, cut into ¼-inch pieces and chilled

1 large egg, chilled

⅓ cup ice water

SUGGESTED FILLINGS

Ham and cheese

Mozzarella, tomato, and basil

Roasted peppers and goat cheese

Roasted vegetable, garbanzo beans (chickpeas), and pesto or tomato sauce

Chicken, spinach, and béchamel sauce

Chocolate and banana

Dulce de leche and peaches or apples

➡ continues

EMPANADAS *continued*

➡ Make the dough: Place the flour in a large bowl that has been refrigerated for 30 minutes. Add the salt and chilled butter. Working quickly, use your fingers or a pastry cutter to rub the butter into the flour until only pea-size pebbles of butter remain. Work the egg and ice water into the flour mixture until it is fully incorporated. Do not worry if some butter pebbles remain. Turn out the dough onto a floured work surface and knead a few times. Form into a disk, wrap tightly in plastic wrap or waxed paper, and refrigerate for at least an hour and up to 8 or freeze for up to 3 months. If freezing, allow the wrapped dough to fully defrost in the refrigerator before proceeding.

➡ To assemble the empanadas: Preheat the oven to 350°F.

➡ Divide the dough into quarters. Roll one of the quarters to a ⅛-inch thickness. Use a biscuit cutter or glass to cut out 4-inch rounds. Repeat with the remaining dough.

➡ Fill the empanadas by topping the bottom half of a dough round with 1 tablespoon of your desired filling, leaving a ¼-inch border. Wet the bottom border with water. Fold the top of the dough round over the filling and press the seam shut. Use a fork to decoratively flute the seam edge. Repeat with the remaining rounds, arranging on a parchment-lined cookie sheet. Brush with egg wash and bake until browned, 20 to 25 minutes.

➡ The cooked and cooled empanadas keep, covered and refrigerated, for up to 3 days, or frozen in an airtight container, for up to 3 months. Defrost in the refrigerator and rewarm at 275°F for 10 minutes.

Frittata

In that frazzled moment when you are running late, everyone in the house is grumpy-hungry and there's "not a thing in the fridge," the answer is always: frittata. It is fast, filling, and will take on any ingredients you have on hand. Some grated cheese, a little chopped ham, a few strips of bacon, a link or two of sausage, one or two potatoes, a little cooked veg, canned artichokes, smoked salmon, frozen peas, an onion, a tomato, just some herbs—any of these, or a combination, will do. That, plus a dozen eggs (or nearly a dozen), and this family meal is within our grasp anytime.

➡ *continues*

FRITTATA *continued*

Makes 4 to 6 servings

10 large eggs

½ cup milk

½ teaspoon salt

Freshly ground black pepper

2 tablespoons unsalted butter or olive oil

1 onion, diced

1 to 2 cups of any type of frittata fillers that you like (cheese, such as crumbled feta,

   grated Cheddar or Swiss, or hunks of creamy goat; cooked meat, such as bits of chicken,

   salmon, ham, bacon, or sausage; any sort of steamed, roasted, or grilled vegetables, roughly

   chopped; little treats, such as canned artichokes or olives; handfuls of minced fresh herbs)

➡ In a medium-size bowl, whisk the eggs until pale yellow. Add the milk, salt, and a few grinds of pepper to taste. Set aside.

➡ Preheat the broiler.

➡ Heat a medium-size sauté pan over medium heat until a drop of water dances on its surface. Add the butter and swirl to coat the pan. Add the onion, season with salt, and sauté until translucent, 3 to 5 minutes. Add the egg mixture and strew the ingredients of your choice evenly across the mixture. Gently swirl the pan and tap down any chunky ingredients to ensure that they are all coated with the egg mixture. Cook on medium heat, gently lifting up the edges of the frittata to allow the liquid egg mixture to flow underneath the cooked egg on the bottom of the pan. When the frittata has a 1-inch border of firm egg mixture around its perimeter, transfer it to the broiler, setting the pan 3 to 4 inches below the element. Broil until the eggs are cooked through and lightly browned on top, about 5 minutes. Remove from the heat and allow to rest for 5 minutes.

➡ Place a plate or cutting board on top of the cooked frittata. Place your nondominant hand on top of the plate, press firmly, and quickly and confidently invert the frittata onto it. Cut into wedges and serve hot or at room temperature. The frittata keeps at room temperature for up to 2 hours or, cooled, covered, and refrigerated, for up to 3 days.

Enchiladas

Melted cheese makes everything taste great. Enchiladas, generously stuffed tortillas, enveloped in a tangy sauce, all under a blanket of bubbly cheese, are a real crowd-pleaser. A casserole dish of them goes a long way, making this a solid contender for a potluck dish or one to share with friends. You can use any leftovers you have on hand in the filling.

Makes 6 servings

4 tablespoons olive oil

1 onion, diced

Salt and freshly ground black pepper

2 garlic cloves, minced

1 tablespoon mild chili powder

1 tablespoon ground cumin

1 quart (32 ounces) whole canned tomatoes (preferably home-canned), pureed

2 cups leftovers (such as cooked meat, fish, chicken, or cooked vegetables),
    cut into bite-size pieces if necessary

2 cups cooked or canned beans, drained and rinsed

2 cups shredded Cheddar cheese

12 (6-inch) corn or flour tortillas

Garnishes, such as sour cream, pickled jalapeños, or minced fresh cilantro (optional)

➡ Preheat the oven to 350°F.

➡ Sauté the onion, seasoned with salt, in 2 tablespoons of the olive oil over medium heat until translucent, 3 to 5 minutes. Add the garlic and sauté until fragrant, about 1 minute. Add a few grinds of pepper, the chili powder, and the cumin and give it a stir. Add the tomatoes and simmer until thickened, 10 to 15 minutes.

➡ Meanwhile, heat a medium-size sauté pan over medium heat. Add the remaining 2 tablespoons of oil, the leftovers, and beans and sauté until heated through, about 5 minutes. Add 1 cup of the tomato mixture and 1 cup of the cheese and stir to combine. Set aside.

➡ continues

➡ Coat the bottom of a 9 by 12-inch casserole dish with 1 cup of the tomato mixture. Fill a tortilla with ⅓ cup of the bean mixture and roll to secure the filling. Place in the casserole dish, seam side down. Hold the filled tortilla with tongs and use it to "mop" a little of the sauce on the bottom of the dish to coat the sides of the tortilla. Continue with the remaining tortillas. Add ¼ cup of water to the remaining sauce and pour it over the filled tortillas. Top with the remaining cup of cheese. Bake until hot and bubbling, 25 to 30 minutes. Serve, passing garnishes if you like.

➡ The casserole can be made, but not baked, up to 8 hours ahead. The baked casserole keeps, cooled, covered, and refrigerated, for up to 3 days.

Risotto

Risotto is one of those dishes that sound fancy but is deeply rooted in good, honest peasant food (my favorite!). This creamy, cheesy dish will take on the personality of whatever ingredients you have on hand. Start with the base—rice, stock, and cheese—and stud this luscious porridge with just a handful of meat, fish, or vegetables for a rustically elegant meal.

Note: If you have the good fortune to have leftover risotto, make risotto cakes. Press the cold rice into patties. Dip each patty into beaten egg and then bread crumbs (see page 184). Sauté lightly in olive oil. Serve on a salad for a knockout starter or come-over-for-lunch showstopper.

Makes 4 servings with leftovers

2 quarts chicken or vegetable stock (for homemade, see pages 142 and 107)

¼ cup olive oil

2 cups Arborio rice

1 onion, finely diced

➡ *continues*

RISOTTO *continued*

Salt and freshly ground black pepper

2 garlic cloves, minced

1 teaspoon dried thyme

1 cup white wine

2 cups leftovers of your choice (such as any cooked meat, fish, or vegetables), diced

8 ounces Parmigiano-Reggiano cheese, grated (about 2 cups)

- In a medium-size saucepan, bring the stock to a simmer. Keep warm over low heat.
- In a 6-quart Dutch oven or other heavy-bottomed pot, heat the oil over medium heat. Add the rice and sauté until the rice is opaque, stirring frequently. Add the onion, season with salt and pepper, and sauté until translucent, 3 to 5 minutes, stirring frequently to prevent sticking. Add the garlic and thyme and sauté until fragrant, about a minute more.
- Add the wine and simmer, stirring constantly, until the liquid is absorbed. Add the stock, 1 cup at a time, stirring constantly, until all liquid has been absorbed before adding more. As you near the end of the stock, test the rice for doneness (some batches will take more or less liquid than the others). A grain, bitten in half, should be translucent all the way through with no opaque grit in the middle. When you reach this stage, add the leftovers you will be using and stir to heat through.
- Remove the risotto from the heat and add half of the cheese, stirring to combine. The risotto should be rich and creamy. Thin the risotto, if necessary, with a little extra stock or water to reach the desired consistency. Divide among four bowls, topping with extra cheese.

Fried Rice

Not only is this one of the best ways to use leftover cooked rice, rice that has been cooked, cooled, and refrigerated is the essential ingredient—freshly cooked, hot rice will clump and go gooey. So, say you're using up leftovers or that you planned it this way. Either way, it's a tasty side dish or, loaded with plenty of goodies, a super lunch or light supper. My favorite version uses left-over, flaked, cooked salmon, but any cooked fish, vegetables, or meat would do—even crumbled sausage or leftover burger patties. You really can't mess this thing up.

Makes 4 servings

2 tablespoons neutral oil, such as organic canola

2 large eggs, lightly beaten

1 onion, diced

1 garlic clove, minced

1 tablespoon minced fresh ginger

2 cups cold, cooked rice

¼ cup soy sauce

1 to 2 cups assorted leftovers (such as cooked meat, fish, or veg; salmon and shrimp are super)

2 scallions, chopped (optional)

→ Heat a large sauté pan over high heat until a drop of water dances across its surface. Add the oil and swirl to coat the bottom of the pan. Add the eggs and gently scramble them with a fork. Remove the eggs from the pan and set aside.

→ Add the onion and sauté until it begins to brown at the edges, about 3 minutes. Add the garlic and ginger and sauté for 30 seconds. Add the rice, breaking it up with your hands, if necessary, and sauté for 1 to 2 minutes, adding a splash of water if it begins to stick. Pour the soy sauce over the heated rice, add the leftovers and the scallions, if using, and stir to heat through. Return the egg to the rice mixture, chopping it up with your fork or spatula and stir it into the mixture. Serve immediately.

METRIC CONVERSIONS

Equivalents and Metric Conversions

The recipes in this book have not been tested with metric measurements, so some variations might occur.

Remember that the weight of dry ingredients varies according to the volume or density factor: 1 cup of flour weighs far less than 1 cup of sugar, and 1 tablespoon doesn't necessarily hold 3 teaspoons.

General Formula for Metric Conversion	
Ounces to grams	multiply ounces by 28.35
Grams to ounces	multiply ounces by 0.035
Pounds to grams	multiply pounds by 453.5
Pounds to kilograms	multiply pounds by 0.45
Cups to liters	multiply cups by 0.24
Fahrenheit to Celsius	subtract 32 from Fahrenheit temperature, multiply by 5, divide by 9
Celsius to Fahrenheit	multiply Celsius temperature by 9, divide by 5, add 32

Weight (Mass) Measurements

1 ounce = 30 grams

2 ounces = 55 grams

3 ounces = 85 grams

4 ounces = ¼ pound = 125 grams

8-ounces = ½ pound = 240 grams

12 ounces = ¾ pound = 375 grams

16 ounces = 1 pound = 454 grams

Linear Measurements

½ in = 1½ cm

1 inch = 2½ cm

6 inches = 15 cm

8 inches = 20 cm

10 inches = 25 cm

12 inches = 30 cm

20 inches = 50 cm

Oven Temperature Equivalents, Fahrenheit (F) and Celsius (C)

100°F = 38°C

200°F = 95°C

250°F = 120°C

300°F = 150°C

350°F = 180°C

400°F = 205°C

450°F = 230° C

Volume (Dry) Measurements

¼ teaspoon = 1 milliliter

½ teaspoon = 2 milliliters

¾ teaspoon = 4 milliliters

1 teaspoon = 5 milliliters

1 tablespoon = 15 milliliters

¼ cup = 59 milliliters

⅓ cup = 79 milliliters

½ cup = 118 milliliters

⅔ cup = 158 milliliters

¾ cup = 177 milliliters

1 cup = 225 milliliters

4 cups or 1 quart = 1 liter

½ gallon = 2 liters

1 gallon = 4 liters

Volume (Liquid) Measurements

1 teaspoon = ⅙ fluid ounce = 5 milliliters

1 tablespoon = ½ fluid ounce = 15 milliliters

2 tablespoons = 1 fluid ounce = 30 milliliters

¼ cup = 2 fluid ounces = 60 milliliters

⅓ cup = 2 ⅔ fluid ounces = 79 milliliters

½ cup = 4 fluid ounces = 118 milliliters

1 cup or ½ pint = 8 fluid ounces = 250 milliliters

2 cups or 1 pint = 16 fluid ounces = 500 milliliters

4 cups or 1 quart = 32 fluid ounces = 1,000 milliliters

1 gallon = 4 liters

RESOURCES

Composting

Let It Rot!: The Gardener's Guide to Composting
   Stu Campbell, Storey Publishing, 1998
   All of the basics for your backyard composting.

New York City's Greenmarket Compost Program
   http://www.grownyc.org/compost
   Learn how one city is turning residential food scraps into rich compost.

The Rodale Book of Composting: Easy Methods for Every Gardener
   Grace Gershuny and Deborah L. Martin, Rodale Books 1992

More on Food Waste

*American Wasteland: How America Throws Away Nearly Half Its Food
(and What We Can Do About It)*
   Jonathan Bloom, Da Capo Lifelong Books, 2010
   A primer on the food waste in the United States.

Feedback
   http://feedbackglobal.org/
   The website for Feedback, Tristram Stuart's environmental organization
   that campaigns to end food waste at every level of the food system.

Love Food Hate Waste

http://www.lovefoodhatewaste.com/

UK-based initiative. Good information and you can't beat that charming accent.

Still Tasty

http://www.stilltasty.com/

Interactive shelf-life database.

Waste: Uncovering the Global Food Scandal

Tristram Stuart, W. W. Norton & Company, 2009

The facts and figures of the global waste problem.

Wasted Food

http://www.wastedfood.com/

Jonathan Bloom's website for the latest info and resources for reducing food waste.

Whole Animal Butchery

The Complete Nose to Tail

Fergus Henderson, Ecco, 2013

A gorgeous cookbook for using up all the bits.

The River Cottage Meat Book

Hugh Fearnley-Whittingstall, Ten Speed Press, 2007

Butchering basics and solid recipes.

Whole Beast Butchery: The Complete Visual Guide to Beef, Lamb, and Pork

Ryan Farr and Brigit Binns, Chronicle Books, November 16, 2011

A butchering primer.

Traditional Kitchen Craft

EcoCentric Blog

http://www.gracelinks.org/blog

Information and action plans for more sustainable food, water, and energy systems.

Nourishing Traditions: The Cookbook That Challenges Politically Correct Nutrition and the Diet Dictocrats

Sally Fallon and Mary G. Enig, NewTrends Publishing, 2001

The whys and hows of traditional dishes.

Put 'em Up!

Sherri Brooks Vinton, Storey, 2010

Learn how to can, ferment, dry, and infuse the harvest.

Wild Fermentation

Sandor Ellix Katz, Chelsea Green Publishing, 2003

The master reference on fermentation.

Real Food Movement Backgrounders

Edible Communities

http://www.ediblecommunities.com

A national network of local magazines that point eaters to all the noble, delicious things their communities have to offer.

Environmental Working Group

http://www.ewg.org

A great resource for environmental responsibility. It publishes a yearly shopper's guide and a "dirty dozen" of the twelve most pesticide-laden crops in the produce aisle.

Omnivore's Dilemma
> Michael Pollan, Penguin, 2007
> Thoughtful examination of our modern food system.

The Real Food Revival: Aisle by Aisle, Morsel by Morsel
> Sherri Brooks Vinton and Ann Clark Espuelas, J. P. Tarcher, 2005
> Practical advice for sourcing real, sustainably produced food.

Sustainable Table
> http://www.sustainabletable.org
> An excellent resource on all issues surrounding sustainable agriculture, with a section devoted to food waste.

Sustainable Food Sourcing Guides

Eat Well Guide
> http://www.eatwellguide.org
> This site offers a powerful search engine that allows you to find real food near you!

Eat Wild
> http://www.eatwild.com
> Features the country's most extensive list of suppliers of pasture-raised products.

Monterey Bay Aquarium
> http://www.montereybayaquarium.com
> On this site you can learn more about sustaining life in our waters—an issue that is desperately urgent—and download a pocket guide to eating seafood that is caught responsibly.

ACKNOWLEDGMENTS

Deep gratitude always to my husband, Drew, and my kids, Ava and Thayer—
I quite like you all. Thanks to the Lisa Ekus Group for all of their support.
Thanks to Renée Sedliar and the Perseus team for such great work on the
book.

INDEX

Sherri Brooks Vinton wants you to have a more delicious life. Her writing, talks, and hands-on workshops teach fellow eaters how to find, cook, and preserve local, seasonal, farm friendly food. To find out more about Sherri and a list of current appearances, visit www.sherribrooksvinton.com.

About Sherri

You might expect a food epiphany to strike in the kitchen, at the table, maybe in the market. For Sherri Brooks Vinton, her aha moment came on the back of a motorcycle. A cross-country tour brought her face-to-face with the negative impacts of industrial agriculture and compelled her to trade in her career as a dot-com executive to begin a quest for food raised with integrity.

Sherri's books, lectures, and workshops give fellow eaters the practical information they need to support local agriculture with their food choices. Her first book, *The Real Food Revival: Aisle by Aisle, Morsel by Morsel,* teaches readers how and why to enjoy sustainably raised foods. In her current series of *Put 'em Up!* books, Sherri walks eaters through the preserving processes that allow them to enjoy seasonal foods all year long. Sherri's discussions and workshops on "how to reclaim the food chain" have been offered at a variety of venues including Stone Barns Center for Food and Agriculture and the San Francisco Ferry Plaza Market. She is honored to have been featured on a number of radio and television programs including Martha Stewart Radio and the Leonard Lopate Show with Ruth Reichl. Through a national column for Edible Communities, Sherri has contributed to numerous Edible publications across the country.